Dedication

*To the glory of God
in the salvation of sinners,
and the sanctification of the
saints of God, this volume
is prayerfully dedicated*

ADVENTURES IN FAITH

Studies in the Life of Abraham

Books by M. R. De Haan

M. R. De Haan Classic Library

ADVENTURES IN FAITH

Studies in the Life of Abraham

M. R. De Haan

kregel
PUBLICATIONS

Grand Rapids, MI 49501

Cover photo: Copyright © 1995 Kregel, Inc.
Cover design: Art Jacobs

Library of Congress Cataloging-in-Publication Data
De Haan, M. R. (Martin Ralph), 1891–1964.
  Adventures in faith: studies in the life of Abraham / M. R. De Haan.
      p.   cm. (M. R. De Haan classic library)
  Originally published: Grand Rapids, Mich.: Zondervan Publishing House, 1953.
  1. Abraham (Biblical patriarch). I. Title. II. Series: De Haan, M. R. (Martin Ralph), 1891–1964. M. R. De Haan classic library.
BS580.A3D43   1996   222'.11092—dc20   96-10314
                                    [B]   CIP
ISBN 0-8254-2481-x

        1 2 3 4 5 printing/year 00 99 98 97 96

Contents

Foreword

Salvation is by the grace of God, appropriated by faith in the promises of God and applied to the sinner by the Spirit of God. We are saved by grace, and kept by grace and are all received through simple faith in the Word of the living God. The Bible knows no other salvation than this. No wonder then that the enemy of our souls seeks to corrupt the simple message of faith by the addition of all sorts of human works, religion, ceremony, emotions, and deeds of the law.

Within the past few years there has been a greatly accelerated increase in the number of cults and sects which preach grace plus works, and faith plus human effort. With a prayer that this volume may be blessed by the Holy Spirit in showing many the error of adding man's efforts to the finished work of Christ, this volume on *Adventures In Faith* is sent forth.

The record of Abraham is especially used by the Holy Spirit to instruct us in the life of faith. Abraham is called the "father of the faithful," and the "friend of God." Abraham, however, is not an example of perfect faith, nor of normal faith, but rather a picture of the average life in faith.

An exhaustive treatment of the life of faith of father Abraham would require the writing of innumerable volumes. I have made no attempt to cover every aspect of the life of faith of this patriarch. I have chosen rather some of the high spots in the record, trusting that they will further stimulate readers to a more extensive study of this most interesting Bible character and his instructive history.

Most of the chapters in this book represent radio broadcasts given over the coast-to-coast Mutual network by the author. With a minimum of editing and revision they are now published in this form and in one single volume.

THE AUTHOR

CHAPTER ONE

The Faith of Abraham

> And Terah took Abram his son, and Lot the son of Haran his son's son, and Sarai his daughter in law, his son Abram's wife; and they went forth with them from Ur of the Chaldees, to go into the land of Canaan; and they came unto Haran, and dwelt there.
>
> And the days of Terah were two hundred and five years: and Terah died in Haran (Genesis 11:31-32).

In these verses we are introduced to father Abraham, called in Scripture the "friend of God" and "the father of the faithful." We are introduced to the father of the nation of Israel and the spiritual father of all true believers; to the man who, with his descendants, is the subject of the whole Bible revelation; and who, with his son, Isaac, his grandson, Jacob, and his great grandson, Joseph, dominates all the rest of the book of Genesis. The importance of this man Abraham may be seen in the prominent place which the Holy Spirit gives to him in this first book of the Bible.

Prominence of Abraham and Descendants

Consider the prominence of the record devoted to Abraham. The first two thousand years of human history are all covered in eleven chapters (Genesis 1 to 11). No less than twenty generations — a period of twenty centuries — are covered in these eleven brief chapters. This first section of Genesis, ends at chapter 11, verse 30. The second section of Genesis begins with the record of Abraham. All the rest of the Book of Genesis from chapter 12 to 50, covering a period of only about four hundred years, is entirely devoted to the history of Abraham, Isaac, Jacob, and Abraham's great grandson, Joseph. The rest of the Old Testament, the entire thirty-nine books, deals with the history of the nation which sprang from Abraham, the nation of Israel. All the rest of the entire Bible is occupied with and centers in Abraham's greater Son, the Lord Jesus Christ.

I state these simple facts at the outset of this series of messages on Abraham to emphasize the important, strategic place he holds in the revelation of God's plan of salvation. There are only four men who dominate the greater part of the first book of the Bible, and their descendants dominate the entire Scriptures. In the history of these four men we see God's wonderful plan of redemption. The theme of the Bible is salvation through grace, appropriated by faith. While the Bible contains a great deal of information concerning various subjects such as history, geography, geology, the customs and habits of people, chemistry and almost every other subject, these subjects are only introduced to reveal the plan of salvation and because they have some bearing on the revelation of God's plan of redemption.

BOOK OF REDEMPTION

The answer to the question, Why the unusual prominence given to Abraham and his son, grandson, and great grandson, in the greater part of Genesis, and his descendants in the entire Bible is evident when we remember why the Bible was written. We repeat, the Bible is a book of redemption, and God's plan of redemption must come through this nation which sprang from these four men, for "salvation is of the Jews." It was through this nation, Israel, the seed of Abraham, that God in His sovereign purpose was to give us our Bible, His own revelation, and through this nation He was to give us our Saviour, the Lord Jesus Christ. For this reason the Holy Spirit devoted only eleven chapters to the first two thousand years of human history. God wastes no time with the past, but speaks almost entirely concerning the future. This will be clear to you when I simply remind you that only one verse in the entire Bible is devoted to telling us all that God wants us to know about where the world came from, and only one chapter in the Bible to telling us where we human beings came from. All the rest of Scripture deals with the future of the world, and where we are going to spend eternity.

The first verse of the Bible consisting of only seven words in the original and only ten in the English Bible is all that is needed for God to tell us how the world began. That verse, you remember, is:

> In the beginning God created the heaven and the earth (Genesis 1:1).

This is the whole and entire revelation of God concerning the origin of this earth. The rest of the Bible is occupied with the future of this world.

NATURAL MAN CONCERNED WITH PAST ONLY

The record of our origin is also brief. A few verses in Genesis 2 tell us how we were created and where we came from. Here is God's brief record of that incident:

> And the Lord God formed man of the dust of the ground, and breathed into his nostrils the breath of life; and man became a living soul (Genesis 2:7).

That is practically the entire story in one verse. There, in twenty-seven simple words, we have all God wants us to know regarding our origin. Again, the rest of the Bible is concerned with where we are going.

God wants us to prepare for the future, not to ponder over the distant, musty past. The past seems to be unimportant in the estimate of God; the future is the important issue. But sinful, natural man turns this truth completely around. The natural man is intensely concerned about the origin of the earth, but pays little attention to where it is heading. He searches the heavens with his telescope, digs into the earth with his spade, burrows through the rocks with his drill, examines the earth in the crucible and test tube and splits the atom. As he engages in his frantic search into the realm of astronomy, archaeology, geology, chemistry and physics to try to find out how and when the earth came into being.

What does he come up with? A thousand foolish theories of evolution. He invents the nebular hypothesis, discards it; invents the primordial cell theory, discards it; then invents the fire-mist theory, and a hundred others. He writes volumes and fills huge libraries full of books and articles on evolution, on the origin of things, on the origin of the species and of the earth, and on the age of the earth. All this time the natural man gives but little thought to the future, makes no preparation for eternity, has no interest in his future abode and refuses to study the one Book which can tell him about these things. Thus he speeds on to an endless, eternal hell.

The natural man has the same reckless concern about the origin of man. Instead of searching the Scriptures for God's plan for his own eternal future, he neglects all this and spends his time trying to find out where he came from. What does he come up with this time? Evolution again. He expects us to believe that man began as a little cell; that the cell became a plant; the plant became a fish; the fish began to fly; the bird lost its feathers, grew hair and climbed a tree; the monkey lost his tail and much of his hair; and the result was man.

BIBLE EASIER TO BELIEVE

I submit to you that a comparison of this theory of evolution with the simple record of the Word of God concerning the origin of man will show the folly of man's speculations. God says:

> In the beginning God created the heaven and the earth (Genesis 1:1).

> So God created man in his own image, in the image of God created He him (Genesis 1:27).

It is a thousand times easier to believe this statement of Genesis than to believe the theories of so-called science. Moreover, God expects us to believe His Word. He will not condescend to argue with an infinitesimal speck of dust such as we are to explain the how and the why of a sovereign Creator's dealings. What silly presumption to call in question the Creator, as though He would have to give an account to us of how and why and when He did as He did. His Word is: "In the beginning God created." Take it or leave it.

If we can believe that opening statement, we can believe everything else in the Bible. If we can believe that God, all alone from a beginningless eternity, could suddenly speak one single word, and by that word create the universe out of nothing, and set it moving in order and precision with all the laws governing its course—if we can believe that, we can believe anything He says. Then we can believe that He could part the sea, walk on the waters, still the storm, cast out demons, make iron to swim, change water to wine, and make a whale to swallow a man and cause it to cast the man out alive after three days.

Now you may ask, "What has all this to do with Abraham?" I have said all this to show you the reason that God gives such prominence to Abraham and his three generations of descendants in the Book of Genesis. We repeat, the Bible is a book of salvation, and gives us a minimum of the past and deals predominantly with the future, the all-important future, eternity.

THE PLAN OF SALVATION

Now in the history of Abraham, Isaac, Jacob and Joseph, God reveals this plan of future salvation. In this plan are four important steps. I believe they are given in Romans 8:28 to 31. In verse 28 Paul tells us:

> And we know that all things work together for good to them

that love God, to them who are the called according to his
purpose.
God has a purpose in view in the salvation of every believer,
and everything which happens to a believer is part of a definite
plan to bring the final purpose to pass.

In verse 29 Paul tells us what this purpose is:

> For whom he did foreknow, he also did predestinate to be
> conformed to the image of his Son, that he might be the first-
> born among many brethren.

God's purpose is ultimately to make every child of God just
like the Lord Jesus. Before God is through with His children,
every one of them will be like the Saviour Himself. Paul
here is thinking of those who are already saved, and says that
God has predestinated them to become like His Son, and that
all things which He sends into or permits in their lives are His
own work of accomplishing this one great end. That all
their trials and testings are but God's way of conforming His
children to His own image is a comforting truth to know.
As the Christian lies upon his bed of suffering, passes through
trials, experiences loss and pain and sorrow, God knows about
it all and will make all this only a means of making him like
Jesus.

In the next verse, verse 30, we come to the steps in this
process. In Romans 8:28 we learn that God has a purpose
with believers. In Romans 8:29 we learn what that purpose
is and that believers are predestinated for it. Then in verse
30 we read:

> Moreover whom he did predestinate, them he also called:
> and whom he called, them he also justified: and whom he justi-
> fied, them he also glorified.

Notice in this passage four words, four steps in salvation:

1. Predestination
2. Calling
3. Justification
4. Glorification

According to this passage, salvation begins in God with pre-

destination and ends in Christ in glorification. Between these
there is calling and justification.

Four Steps — Four Men

Now to return to Abraham, I am sure that Paul must have
had in mind the four men in Genesis who completely dominate the book from chapter 11 to 50; for these four men correspond exactly to these four steps of faith. Abraham is the
great example of divine, sovereign predestination. Isaac becomes the great example of divine calling. You will remember
that Ishmael, the firstborn of Abraham, was Abraham's
choice, but God said, "In Isaac shall thy seed be called." So
we see that "whom he did predestinate, them he also called."
Then we come to Jacob, the great example of divine justification. Jacob certainly had nothing to commend him to Almighty
God. He was justified by divine grace alone. God Himself
said, "Jacob have I loved, but Esau have I hated." Then follows Joseph, the great example of glorification. Sold by his
brethren and left for dead, he becomes ruler of Egypt at the
right hand of the king. In these four men, therefore, we have
a perfect picture of the four steps of salvation: predestination,
calling, justification and glorification.

I want to press again upon each one of you the necessity
of a personal acceptance of this grace of God. I said, that
depraved man delves only into the past, while God wants
us to think of our future. May I ask you, How much thought
have you given to your future? Only a few more days or years
at the most before you must leave this life. What then? Then
an endless eternity. Oh, my friend, be wise and think of the
future, and follow the example of Abraham of whom it is said
that he considered himself only a pilgrim and stranger here
below and "looked for a city which hath foundations, whose
builder and maker is God."

CHAPTER TWO

The Objects of Faith

> And Joshua said unto all the people, Thus saith the Lord God of Israel, Your fathers dwelt on the other side of the flood in old time, even Terah, the father of Abraham, and the father of Nachor: and they served other gods.
>
> And I took your father Abraham from the other side of the flood, and led him throughout all the land of Canaan, and multiplied his seed, and gave him Isaac (Joshua 24:2-3).

According to this Scripture, God called Abraham in sovereign grace. Man had utterly failed after the flood of Noah, and God now abandons the nations and gives them up to themselves. He steps aside to choose one man in sovereign grace. Through him, his son Isaac and his grandson Jacob, He begins an entirely new work. Through Abraham and his seed He is to give the revelation of His will in the Scriptures, and out of Abraham and his seed is to come the Saviour.

Now the story of Abraham was given to us to illustrate God's plan of salvation. It is more than the history of a man and his descendants, interesting as that may be. In Abraham, Isaac, Jacob and Joseph, who with their descendants dominate the entire Bible, we have a revelation of the message of the grace of God. In the former chapter we quoted Romans 8:28 and 29 and pointed out that God has determined and predestinated every believer in the Lord Jesus, and that before God is through with him, He is going to make him just like Jesus. God never will stop until He accomplishes that purpose. God seems to say, "I'm not going to leave a single stone unturned, I'm not going to leave a thing undone, even though it may mean pain and tragedy and suffering and tears and heartbreak and bereavement and death, or even the judgment seat of Christ, until you become like my Son." This purpose is fixed and this destiny is determined beforehand. That is the meaning of the word "predestinate."

As an illustration of how God accomplishes this purpose, we have the example of Abraham. God had to make him like His Son, and it was a long and a painful process. From Genesis 12 through 22, where the process finally reaches the peak of victory and faith in Abraham's sacrifice of his son Isaac, we have God dealing in grace with Abraham, making him more like Himself. When God began to deal with him, He did not stop until He had accomplished His purpose. Sometimes it meant to Abraham failure, hardship, heartbreak. It meant pulling his heart out of his very breast; it meant stumbling at times; yea, it even meant years out of fellowship with God; but all of this testing had its part in the overruling wisdom and foreknowledge of God in finally accomplishing what He had set out to do with Abraham when He called him out of Ur of the Chaldees.

ABRAHAM — PREDESTINATION

Abraham is the great example of divine, sovereign election and predestination. He was not a Jew when God called him. He was not even a Hebrew. He was a pagan. At the beginning of this chapter stands a verse from Joshua, chapter 24, where the recorder tells us that Abraham came from an idolatrous family. Passing by the whole nation of Chaldeans, God goes to one single family, and in that one family He passes by all except one man, Abraham, and says to him: "I will make of thee a great nation." Such action on the part of God is nothing else but sovereign grace. There was certainly nothing in Abraham. God did not see a thing in him that made him worthy of being called rather than others; but in sovereign, absolute sovereign grace, He chose Abraham, according to His own purpose. Abraham, then, becomes the great example of divine predestination.

Isaac — Calling

We have the second step in the plan of salvation in this passage: "Whom he did predestinate, them he also called." Isaac is the great example of effective, divine calling. You will recall how Abraham could not wait for God's promised son to come. Taking matters into his own hands, he raised up a son of the flesh and called his name Ishmael. Even though Abraham had set his heart upon this son, God said, "In Isaac shall thy seed be called." God sets aside the oldest, and takes the youngest. The first becomes last, and the last must be the first. In nature, of course, the reverse is always true. The first is always first with us, and we cannot change it. That is the natural order. One is one, and two comes after one. But in grace God always upsets nature, and turns it up-side-down. God makes the last to become first, and the first to become the last. In grace two always comes before one. So He took Isaac, the second, and said, "In Isaac shall thy seed be called." "For whom he did predestinate, them he also called."

Jacob — Justification

Coming to the third of the patriarchs, Jacob, we find that he is the example of divine justification. Jacob, the crook, the rascal, the cheat, the liar, the thief, the conniver, the sup-planter, becomes the example of justification. That really is something divine. "For whom he called, them he also justi-fied." Why did God choose Jacob? Certainly not on the basis of his worth; certainly not on the basis of his own merit. Then on what basis did He call him? It was again on the basis of sovereign grace, appropriated through faith.

Esau was a gentleman compared with Jacob. Esau was a home-loving boy, kind to his father as far as the record goes.

When Isaac, the old man, wanted comfort in his old age, he called Esau, not Jacob. He calls the gentle Esau and says, "Go and get me some venison and cook it like only you can." And Esau says, "All right, Dad, anything I can do for you." You may search the record and you will find nothing derogatory to Esau, except that he sold his birthright and despised the promise of God. But from every other standpoint, morally and otherwise, there is nothing bad recorded about Esau. He was a pretty good fellow, as fellows go. But now look at Jacob. He schemed with his mother, took the goat skins about his neck to fool his father, and when poor, old, blind Isaac becomes suspicious, Jacob tells a brazen, bold-faced lie and says, "Don't worry, I wouldn't tell you a lie." It was Jacob who stole the birthright from his brother Esau, cheated his father, connived with his mother and then ran away to Padan-Aram and well-nigh ruined his uncle Laban. But he was justified rather than Esau.

Jacob is the kind of person God justifies. God does not save good people. A man must be a sinner to be saved. He has to be absolutely helpless before God can do anything with him. Grace is favor to the unworthy, and the more unworthy a man is, the greater he needs the grace of God. That is why the Lord chose folks like you and me — not because we were better, but in spite of what we are. God's grace is exalted, not in choosing nice people, but taking "not many noble, not many great." God has taken the foolish things of this world, the base things of this world, because of His grace. Thus He steps aside again from the natural course of things and puts aside Esau, the eldest, first from the human standpoint. Of course, Esau deserved to lose his birthright from the standpoint of human responsibility, for he despised it; but that is the human side. Paul, however, is not talking about the human side in Romans 8. He is dealing with sovereign grace. In grace God chose Jacob, good-for-nothing Jacob, because he believed the promise, which belief was also a matter of grace. "Whom he did predestinate, them he also called: and whom he called, them he also justified."

JOSEPH — GLORIFICATION

The last step of salvation reads this way: "Whom he justified, them he also glorified." This brings us to the history of Joseph. Joseph, despised, cast into a pit, sold for twenty pieces of silver into the hands of the heathen, goes into Egypt. There he is exalted at the right hand of the king and glorified exceedingly.

Beginning, then, with God's eternal, sovereign purpose in Abraham, and ending with glorification in Joseph, we have predestination, calling, justification and glorification. It is no wonder that Paul continues in Romans 8:31, 32:

> What shall we then say to these things? If God be for us, who can be against us?
> He that spared not his own Son, but delivered him up for us all, how shall he not with him also freely give us all things?

What God begins He will surely finish.

Now there comes an interesting verse. Romans 8:33:

> Who shall lay anything to the charge of God's elect? It is God that justifieth.

If it is true that whom He did predestinate, them he called, and justified, and also glorified, then certainly there is none that can lay anything to the charge of God's elect; for it is God who justifieth. It is God Himself who has declared the sinner righteous through faith. To support his point further, Paul adds another question and answer in verse 34:

> Who is he that condemneth? It is Christ that died, yea rather, that is risen again, who is even at the right hand of God, who also maketh intercession for us.

It is interesting to note in your Bible that a number of words in these two verses are in italics. For instance, take the passage in Romans 8:33. You will notice that the two words, "it is," are in italics. This means that they have been supplied by the translators. We can better render the verse as follows: "Who shall lay anything to the charge of God's elect? God that justifieth?" Or take verse 34. Leaving out the italicized words, it reads: "Who is he that condemneth? Christ that died, yea rather, that is risen again, who is even at the right hand of God, who also maketh intercession for us?" Paul seems to say, "Do you think that He who chose you and called you and justified you is going to stop short of glorification? Do you think that He is going to condemn you?"

We are not surprised that Paul ends his questioning by crying out in verse 35:

> Who shall separate us from the love of Christ? shall tribulation, or distress, or persecution, or famine, or nakedness, or peril, or sword?

Paul states the same truth positively in II Timothy 1:12:

> I am persuaded that he is able to keep that which I have committed unto him against that day.

Yes salvation is all of the Lord.

CHAPTER THREE

The Demand of Faith

> By faith Abraham, when he was called to go out into a place which he should after receive for an inheritance, obeyed; and he went out, not knowing whither he went.
> By faith he sojourned in the land of promise, as in a strange country, dwelling in tabernacles with Isaac and Jacob, the heirs with him of the same promise:
> For he looked for a city which hath foundations, whose builder and maker is God (Hebrews 11:8-10).

I have called this series of messages *Adventures In Faith*, for truly the Christian walk of faith is full of adventures, full of pleasant, thrilling surprises as we behold God's marvelous providence and His leading of all those who, like Abraham, dare to step out in faith upon His promises. Faith suggests adventure; for faith goes forward, not knowing fully what lies ahead. If we could look ahead, we should not need faith; for then we would walk by sight, and not by faith. The Christian life, therefore, is an adventure, a continual experience of new and thrilling revelations of God's faithfulness, providence and love.

ABRAHAM THE FAITHFUL

The patriarch, Abraham, father of the nation of Israel, and the friend of God, is the great example of the walk of faith in Scripture. He is mentioned over and over again by the writers of the Bible as an example of the growth and victory of real faith. James, Paul, the author of Hebrews and others refer us to the history of this man Abraham when they seek an illustration of saving, working faith. The history of this man begins way back in Genesis 11. After God had given up the wicked nations of the world, He calls this man by sovereign grace to leave his home, his kindred and his friends and to walk alone with Him. The record is rather brief, but full of instruction and profit. After a brief genealogy of Abraham, Moses introduces our hero in Genesis 11:31 as follows:

> And Terah took Abram his son, and Lot the son of Haran his son's son, and Sarai his daughter in law, his son Abram's wife; and they went forth with them from Ur of the Chaldees, to go into the land of Canaan; and they came into Haran, and dwelt there.

GOD FINDS THE SINNER

Notice first of all where God found Abram. It was in Ur of the Chaldees, far, far from the promised land. "Ur" means flame. "Chaldee" means destruction. Literally, then, God found Abram in the place of the flame and in the land of destruction. We call attention to this because the story of Abram is the example of salvation first of all by faith. Abram is first of all an example of the sinner saved by the grace of God. In the place of the flame, in the place of judgment, in the land of destruction is exactly where God finds every sinner whom He saves. By our first birth, like Abram, we were alienated from God, placed under the judgment of hell, and set on an earth destined and doomed to destruction. Moreover, Abram was an idolater. He came from a pagan country and from a pagan nation and from a pagan home. His family worshipped idols, and estranged themselves from the one true God. Joshua gives us this little bit of information in Joshua 24:2. In speaking to Israel he says:

> Thus saith the Lord God of Israel, Your fathers dwelt on the other side of the flood in old time, even Terah, the father of Abraham, and the father of Nachor: and they served other gods.

That, then, is the picture of the sinner, alienated from God, a stranger to the promises and the covenants of God, living under judgment and doomed to destruction. This man, this sinner, God purposed to save by His grace through faith, and called him to leave his old life and to walk by faith and faith alone. Hebrews tells us that Abraham knew not where he was going. He was merely expected to go day by day as the Lord led him in the path of faith.

INCOMPLETE OBEDIENCE

Abram believed God and set out. But then a strange thing happened. He started for the promised land of Canaan, and had gone about one half the distance, when God suddenly stopped him short. We read in Genesis 11:31:

> And they went forth with them from Ur of the Chaldees, to go into the land of Canaan; and they came unto Haran, and dwelt there.

Notice, their goal was Canaan, the promised land of victory; but they came to Haran instead, only about one half the distance to their destination. There they stopped, and as far as we can determine, they spent about six years in this place of desolation. "Haran" means dry, or parched, and fruitless. Canaan stands for fruitfulness and for victory. Here in Haran Abram dwelt for six years. From the record, they were wholly wasted years. There is no record that Abram built any altars here, or that he ever prayed. There is no record of any revelation or encouragement from God, no appearances of the Lord, no victory, no progress, no growth. What a picture of many a Christian who starts out with enthusiasm only to come to a dead standstill before he reaches the place of real victory. Instead of victory, he comes to the place where God must deal with him in judgment, as though he had never even known the Lord.

OLD MAN MUST GO

Now the reason for Abram's wasted years and for God's halting him at Haran is given to us clearly in Genesis 12.

Abram had believed God and gone out of Ur of the Chaldees. So far everything is good. He is out of the city of the flame, and he is away from the land of destruction. But Abram had not fully obeyed God's word, and therefore he must now learn an important lesson in the adventure of faith. He was out of Ur, but Ur was not yet out of him. All this is made clear in Genesis 12:1:

> Now the Lord had said unto Abram, Get thee out of thy country, and from thy kindred, and from thy father's house, unto a land that I will shew thee.

Notice carefully, "Now the Lord had said unto Abram, Get thee out." But from the verses in Genesis 11, we learn that Abram had failed to do this. Instead he took with him his father, Terah, and his nephew, Lot. God had distinctly told Abram to leave his kindred and friends; two things, the world and the flesh. The country represents the world about him; his father and Lot were types of the flesh. Both must be left behind.

While Abram left his country, he nevertheless took the flesh along. For this reason God interrupts His child, to teach him the lesson of separation. Salvation is by faith and faith alone, but if there is to be progress and growth, blessing and victory, there must be separation from the world and from the flesh. That is the next step after conversion. After God had said, "Let there be light," on the first day of creation, He performed an act of separation on the second day -- separation of the waters above the earth and upon the earth. The greatest need of the church and of Christians today is to learn the lesson of separation from the world and from the flesh. Thousands of Christians are at a dead standstill (like Abram in Haran), groping in doubt and fear and uncertainty, having made no progress because of the fleshly habits and sins in their lives.

The Old Must Die

Now see how God deals with the problem of the flesh in the life of Abram. Abram had trusted God and had gone out of Ur, but in disobedience to God's clear instructions had taken his father and Lot along. "Get thee out from thy kindred, and from thy father's house" had been the word of the Almighty. Terah, Abram's father, represents the old man of the flesh. "Terah" means delay. "Haran" means fruitless. Six years Abram lived with Terah in Haran, delayed in a fruitless land; six years of no progress, no growth, no joy or victory. Then we read:

> And the days of Terah were two hundred and five years: and Terah died in Haran (Genesis 11:32).

Terah died in Haran. Thank God, the old man died. Abram must sever the tender ties of the flesh before he can proceed to the place of victory and promise. There is to be a burial in Haran, a blessed funeral. Terah died, and was buried in Haran, the place of fruitlessness. It must have been hard for Abram, but it must be, before he can go on. How much easier it would have been for Abram to have left his father behind in Ur of the Chaldees than to bury him here in a strange land. How much better to obey God willingly and immediately, by separation from the world and the flesh, rather than to disobey and thus to bring God's judgment into our lives, a punishment more painful and lasting than the momentary soreness caused by separation from the world and the flesh.

Having been compelled to obey, Abram finally departs from Haran. He has renounced the flesh and is now ready to go forward. This time he and his family reach their goal and their destination. In Genesis 12:5 we read this:

> And Abram took Sarai his wife, and Lot his brother's son, and all their substance that they had gathered, and the souls that they had gotten in Haran; and they went forth into the land of Canaan; *and into the land of Canaan they came.*

Once before they had started for Canaan, the land of victory, but only went as far as Haran. The old man must first be buried there, and then, significantly, they came into the land of Canaan. Stephen also, in the book of Acts, when speaking of Abraham, says this:

> Then came he out of the land of the Chaldaeans, and dwelt in Charran: and from thence, *when his father was dead,* he removed him into this land, wherein ye now dwell (Acts 7:4).

MORTIFY THE FLESH

Here is a great lesson in the adventure of faith. When we have received Christ we are not any more of this world, but the flesh is still with us and must be dealt with. This was not the only lesson in separation in Abram's life, to be sure. Later on he must separate himself from Lot, then he must sacrifice his own son, Isaac, and finally even Sarah must be buried. Sanctification is not one single spiritual experience, but a series of burials, a succession of funerals, of judgments upon the flesh, or, as Paul puts it, of daily deaths, daily mortifications of the old man and of the flesh and of the world.

Many believers stand in desperate need of just such an experience today. Those whom God has greatly used in the past will testify that, after they were saved, there came a time when God called for a definite surrender of their lives before they could be fully used of Him. Call it whatever you will, but when we definitely obey God in putting away that of which we have been convicted by the Word, there comes a definite blessing and a going forward spiritually. Such an experience, however, happens not once in the Christian's life, but often.

As Abram walked with God he received new light all along the way, which called for new yielding and new obedience as he grew in faith. New obedience came when he separated from Lot, when he refused the spoils of Sodom, when he sacrificed his own son, Isaac. There were blessings all along the way, second, third, fourth and fifth blessings. As often as we follow new light and yield ourselves to His will, we too may experience the fresh blessing of the Almighty.

The rest of the record of Abram in this chapter is precious. He comes to Sichem, the place of strength; then to Moreh, the place of instruction; then to Bethel, the house of God, where God appears again to him, communes with him and renews the covenant. Here Abram builds an altar and calls upon the Name of the Lord. He is now back in full fellowship again, because he has been obedient.

In closing this chapter I would apply this lesson personally to you who are believers. You, too, are saved, but let me ask you, are you making any progress? Do you enjoy your salvation? Is God answering your prayers? Does His Word become more precious to you as you go along? Or, are you unhappy, doubting, fruitless, cold and carnal? Then listen my friend, you need a funeral in your life. There is something that must go, something to be buried before you can go on. Abram was stopped at Haran until Terah died. He had to dig a grave first.

What is it in your own life, Christian, which hinders you and keeps you from the joy of the Christian life? From what do you need to be separated? You know what it is. Is it some secret sin, some habit, some lust, some fleshly thing you are pampering and condoning and excusing? Is it some worldly practice, pride, dishonesty, gossip, an unforgiving spirit, bitterness, a sharp tongue, an uncontrolled and unyielded temper, stubbornness or hatred? Remember, before you can go on, it must go. Terah, the old man, must be buried. Why not stop right now, confess your sin to the Lord Jesus, trust Him to give you the victory, and go on to the place of joy and fruit-bearing? Be honest and put your sin away, turn your life over to Him once and for all and experience the new joy of His presence and fellowship. Dig that grave in Haran now, and go on to the life of victory in Canaan.

CHAPTER FOUR

The Test of Faith

And there was a famine in the land: and Abram went down into Egypt to sojourn there; for the famine was grievous in the land (Genesis 12:10).

There was a famine in the land of plenty, the land flowing with milk and honey, a famine in the land to which Abram had gone in faith and obedience to God's own command and word. Certainly here is a severe test of faith. What an adventure in faith it became before Abram was through. In the previous chapter we saw Abram, the father of the faithful, believing God and leaving his country to go with the Lord to a new and a better land. It is the picture of the believer who trusts God and turns his back on the world to follow Jesus only.

The tie with the flesh is finally broken, the "old man" is left behind, and now Abram moves on to the promised land of Canaan. Along the way he has a few significant experiences. In Genesis 12:6 we learn that he first passes "through the land unto the place of Sichem." "Sichem" is the same as Shechem and means shoulder. The shoulder signifies strength and power and service, for on it the burdens were borne in oriental times. Obedience to God in separation will, therefore, bring power and service. Is your Christian life powerless, drab, and fruitless, my friend? Then ask yourself the question, What is there in my life which is displeasing to God, and must be surrendered and confessed and forsaken, even as in the life

of Abram? God will not bless until we are willing to yield
to His will. As we travel along the highway of the adventures
of faith, we reach many stopping places. As we grow in grace,
as we study His Word, we receive new light concerning things
in our lives that are still wrong. Unless we face each one
of these individually and confess them, we come to a
standstill. The moment we are willing to yield to the new light
that God gives us, He moves us on to the next test; and each
one makes us stronger in the faith. Do not think that victory
and sanctification is a single, isolated experience. It is a growth
in grace and in knowledge. New light reveals new demands
which must be met as we journey on.

ABRAM'S VICTORY

After Abram passed through Sichem, the place of power,
he came to Moreh. "Moreh" means the even place, or the
place of instruction. After Abram's victory at Haran, God
leads him on to the plain of instruction. He needs instruction
for the tests which still lie ahead, for the journey is only just
begun. We read that "the Canaanite was then in the land"
(Genesis 12:6). The Canaanites, who represent the world,
were observing Abram's life and scrutinizing his every
move. They knew that he professed faith in Jehovah, and
they were watching him to see if they could find a flaw in
his profession and faith. How much, therefore, Abram
needed instruction! The world today is also watching the believer and eyeing him closely in order to find some fault, and
so bring reproach upon the cause of the Lord Jesus Christ.
We like Abram should walk carefully, for the Canaanite is
still in the land.

NEW JOYS FOR OBEDIENCE

The Lord comes now to strengthen Abram. He renews His covenant, He encourages His servant. God knows
there are severe tests ahead. He knows how weak His children
are; so He comes to strengthen His servant and give him a
season of rest before applying the next test in the adventure of

faith. We read about the Lord's coming to Abram in that
wonderful eighth verse:

> And he removed from thence unto a mountain on the east
> of Bethel, and pitched his tent, having Bethel on the west, and
> Hai on the east: and there he builded an altar unto the Lord,
> and called upon the name of the Lord.

Perfect communion, blessing and rest in obedience now follow.
Abram was facing Bethel, with his back toward Hai.
"Bethel" means house of God; "Hai" means defeat. Hai was
the city where later Joshua and his armies were defeated because of the disobedience of Achan. So Abram dwells
with his face toward Bethel, the house of God, and his
back toward Hai, the place of defeat. He communes with
God, sacrificing and praying and fellowshipping.

The Next Test

How long Abram dwelt here in peace and quietness we
do not know. The Lord gave him a little season of rest
and refreshing, and then puts His servant to the next great
trial and test. There comes a disturbing situation, a famine in
the land. How it must have troubled Abram. Was he not
where God wanted him? Was he not in the place of fellowship? Then why a famine in the land? It was indeed a great
test of faith, and Abram, we are sorry to say, failed,
miserably failed. Instead of trusting God, he turned to his own
reason, and sought the solution in the arm of the flesh. If
Abram had only trusted God, and said, "God has placed
me here and I am going to stay until He tells me to move,"
God would certainly have honored his faith. He who fed
Elijah by the brook, He who rained manna from heaven
for Abram's descendants, He who filled the disciples' nets
with fish and fed a multitude on a few loaves and fishes,
surely He could take care of Abram also.

Poor Abram, still young in the faith, instead of trusting
God, took matters in his own hands. We read the sad story:

> And there was a famine in the land: and Abram went down

into Egypt to sojourn there; for the famine was grievous in the
land (Genesis 12:10).

Abram went down. He turned his back on Bethel and
went down to Egypt, a country which in the Bible is a type
of the world. The lesson taught here is that it is better to
starve in the place where God wants you to be than to live in
luxury, but not according to the will of God, in Egypt.
Abram was to find this out presently. He was to pay dearly
for his unbelief. In the story we have many, many evidences
of this fact. Abram first of all lost his sense of peace and
security; he began to worry. He feared for Sarai his wife;
for she was very beautiful, and he feared that these conscience-
less Egyptians might kill him and take Sarai. How much
better to have trusted the Lord in Canaan. Abram says to
Sarai:

> When the Egyptians shall see thee . . . they shall say, This
> is his wife: and they will kill me, but they will save thee alive.
> Say, I pray thee, thou art my sister: that it may be well with
> me for thy sake; and my soul shall live because of thee (Genesis
> 12:12-13).

Is this the same man who trusted God, of whom we read,
"He was the friend of God," and "the father of the faithful"?
Yes, it is the same man — none other than this same Abram,
Abram's action only proves how deceitful the flesh is, even
in the believer, and how we ought to be on guard against
it every moment. The Bible knows no such thing as the
eradication of the flesh while we are here below. It is still in
us to overpower us the moment we are off guard and leave the
place of perfect obedience. The saintliest and holiest believer
is not immune to the flesh and temptation, but is all too prone
to yield and submit to it when it appears that obedience to
God may cost him too great a price.

Behold Abram

Behold, therefore, poor Abram. He resorts to lying when
he could have been trusting. He succumbs to fear when he
could have been confident. He makes excuses when he could

have been resting. But worse than that, he was even willing to give his wife, Sarai, to become an adulteress to save his own skin. Believing Sarai to be Abram's sister, the King calls for her and would make her his own wife. How perfectly awful the situation becomes! Is it possible that a believer can fall so low? Yes, indeed it is, and it is an awful price such a believer too must ultimately pay.

Now comes the most wonderful exhibition of the grace of God in behalf of those who belong to Him, even though they are disobedient. While Abram was unfaithful, God remained faithful. We might expect God to say, "Well, Abram, you got yourself into this mess, now you can stew in your own fat. I am going to give you up. I'm all through with you. I'll call somebody else." Did God do anything of the kind? Listen to the record:

> And the Lord plagued Pharaoh and his house with great plagues because of Sarai Abram's wife (Genesis 12:17).

God plagued Pharaoh — not Abram. To be sure, God would deal with Abram also as we will see later, but He would not forsake His child even though the child was living in sin and disobedience. He does not cast the disobedient, sinning believer away, but seeks to bring him back to forgive him and cleanse him. So God plagues Pharaoh's house, until Pharaoh drives Abram and Sarai out of Egypt. God would not leave Abram there, even though He had to use this unbelieving king to drive him back to the place of obedience.

BACK TO BETHEL

Genesis 13 opens with these words:

> And Abram went up out of Egypt, he, and his wife, and all that he had, and Lot with him, into the south.

Abram went up. He is now on the way back, thank God. Ashamed, rebuked, beaten, repentant, he starts back to Bethel. But the damage has been done. He has weakened his testimony and done irreparable damage to weak-kneed, worldly Lot, his nephew. For, mind you, he took Lot along into Egypt. The believer never backslides alone, he always craves company. When a Christian becomes bitter and callous and backslidden, he will always try to make others dissatisfied and critical too. That is the way new sects and denominations have their beginning. One damages not only his own soul when he gets out of fellowship, but he damages other weaker Christians about him. But God brought Abram back, and he comes again to Bethel. Here is the record:

> And he went on his journeys from the south even to Bethel, unto the place where his tent had been at the beginning, between Bethel and Hai;
>
> Unto the place of the altar, which he had made there at the first: and there Abram called on the name of the Lord (Genesis 13:3-4).

How blessed this wonderful record really is! God invites him back into fellowship. Back to Bethel, the house of God.

Have I described your condition right now? You, too, once knew the joy of the Lord, the blessing of fellowship and service in Him. Now you are cold, indifferent, sour and miserable. Oh, come back to Bethel, the place of the altar, which you made there at the first. You, too, have gotten your eyes off the Lord as Abram had, and have gone down into Egypt. You are not happy. You may even imagine the Lord has cast you off, but He has not. He wants you to return. He says:

> If we confess our sins, he is faithful and just to forgive us our sins, and to cleanse us from all unrighteousness (I John 1:9).

Come now; admit your backsliding, confess your sin, return to Him. He will abundantly pardon you. You may again know the joy of the Lord, if you too, like Abram, will only come back to Bethel.

CHAPTER FIVE

The Purposes of God

And there was a famine in the land (Genesis 12:10).

When we are in the place where God wants us, we often expect that God is going to bless us for it. We expect that we are going to be free from all testings and trials. In the life of Abram God makes a great revelation. After a brief respite in the land of Canaan at Bethel, God comes and says, as it were, "Abram, this is only the beginning of your journey of faith. That test I gave you in the past was only to steel and to prepare you, and to make you able to bear even a greater test, and here it is: a famine in the land of plenty."

What does Abram do? He goes down into Egypt. Down, down, down "into Egypt to sojourn there; for the famine was grievous in the land." Abram, the man of faith, failed God. Now God knew that Abram was going to fail, and God could have kept him from failing. God could even have prevented this temptation from coming, but the fact is that God did allow it to come and did permit Abram to fall. We need to recognize this great fundamental truth, that God permitted Abram to be tempted and to fall, knowing that he would make this grievous error and commit a great sin, in order that God might use even this failure and this sin as a means of teaching Abram a still greater lesson which might prevent a still greater tragedy in his life later on.

GOD'S PERMISSIVE WILL

I wonder if we believe that truth. Whether we do or not, it still remains true. God does allow things to come in our

lives. God even allows mistakes to be committed by us in
order that He may use those experiences and mistakes to prevent something more tragic later on. In other words, God can
use "even the wrath of man to praise Him." A couple of
illustrations I am sure, will convince you of the truth of this
fact.

Jacob had eleven sons, ten of whom were out herding the
sheep; one of them, Jacob's favorite, Joseph, was still at home.
His father sent him to his brothers. When his brothers saw
him coming, they put him to death — that at least was their
intent. They put him in a pit, sold him for twenty pieces of
silver, and thought that they had put him out of the way. As
it turned out, he was sold into Egypt. But God in sovereign
wisdom allowed these ten potential murderers to put Joseph to
"death" in order that by that very sin this Joseph might, in
the providence of God, become the savior of the very criminals who had tried to put him to death.

Joseph himself established this fact when he said later:

> Now therefore be not grieved, nor angry with yourselves,
> that ye sold me hither: for God did send me before you to pre-
> serve life (Genesis 45:5).
>
> And God sent me before you to preserve you a posterity in
> the earth, and to save your lives by a great deliverance.
>
> So now it was not you that sent me hither, but God: and
> he hath made me a father to Pharaoh, and lord of all his house,
> and a ruler throughout all the land of Egypt (vss. 7, 8).
>
> But as for you, ye thought evil against me; but God meant
> it unto good, to bring to pass, as it is this day, to save much
> people alive (Genesis 50:20).

Surely here we stand face to face before the revelation of God
that He is able to take the things which men mean for evil,
and make them work out for the good of those whom He has
chosen to love. We would not have you miss those words of
Joseph himself when he says, "And God sent me before you
to preserve you a posterity in the earth," and again in verse
5, "God did send me before you to preserve life." Even

more emphatic is the eighth verse: "So now it was not you that sent me hither, but God."

Come with me to another scene, even to Calvary, for the greatest example of the truth here discussed. See there, hanging upon the Cross of Calvary, the Creator of the universe, sinless, spotless, impeccable. There is pity upon His face and the love of God streaming from His whole being as He hangs there in agony and in blood. His hands and His feet are pierced with cruel nails, his brow with the crown of thorns. His eyes are bloodshot and red, full of agony and pain. His pale, thin lips are pinched with the awful pain of the Cross. Every muscle in His body is tense as the blood oozes from His broken skin. He cries out in His agony to Almighty God, while the angry mob of rebels and bloodthirsty criminals around are demanding His death and are gloating over the death of the sinless Son of God. How in the name of heaven, we ask, can God be up there and see a sight like that, and still keep silence. Why does He not send fire from heaven and plunge these murderers of His Son into an eternal hell forever? Why does He not damn them all? It would have been absolutely just; it would have been righteous for God to do so.

We stand there and cry out, "Oh, God, do something." Instead of doing something, however, God permits these criminals to go right ahead, to crucify His precious Son, until He cries out, "My God, my God, why hast thou forsaken Me?" Instead of helping Him, God turns His back, closes His eyes, blows out the sun, pulls down the curtains of heaven, and allows His Son to suffer innocently and alone, at the hands of these criminals. I hardly know what to say when I realize that God permitted these sinners to kill His Son, in order that by the very death and the murder of His Son He might provide the only way to save the ones who murdered Him. Now that is something to marvel at. He allowed His Son to be murdered because it was the only way that He could save the murderers of His Son.

If God felt that way with Joseph, and with Christ, I think we can understand why He permits things to come into our lives also. Man wants to understand and to reason; he does not want to believe; but when I go to Calvary and stand there and see the Son of God dying in agony and in blood to save me, a good-for-nothing, hell-deserving, rotten, filthy sinner, and to make me a child of God, I ask for no other argument; I ask for no other proof; that is enough for me.

Abram Must Also Trust God

We can also now understand why God permitted Abram to fail, why a famine came in the land of plenty. It was to test Abram and to bring out of it something greater than could have been done in any other way. God seems to test Abram to see whether he will trust God. If Abram had said, "Well, here is a famine and there is all kinds of food in Egypt, but I'm going to trust God alone, I'm going to stay right here, even if I have to starve to death, I'm not going to go, I'm going to stay where God placed me, I'm not going to go until God tells me to go"—if Abram had said that, I am sure that God, who was able to use the ravens to bring the food to Elijah and rain manna from heaven for Israel, would not have failed Abram in this hour. But Abram listened to the flesh and said, "There's all kinds of food in Egypt; here the land is all parched and dry. God wants me to use my head, doesn't He? I'm going to Egypt." And right there he made his mistake. For God after all is faithful. Is it not strange that Abram had trusted God when he left the Ur of the Chaldees and had come all the way to Canaan, but he could not trust God to keep him after he got there? Do you get the point, or shall I make it clearer? Abram trusted God to save him, but he could not trust God to keep him. Regarding his being kept, Abram felt that he had to do something himself. There are thousands of poor souls today who trust God to save their souls, and then think that they have to do the rest. They cannot trust God to keep them, even to the end.

There is another lessson here. We trust God for eternal things, but we do not dare to trust Him for the material. We say, "Amen, hallelujah, Jesus is my Saviour; I know whom I have believed; hallelujah for salvation"; but the moment something goes wrong, all our joy is gone. One of the family gets sick; then we begin to doubt, and cannot trust the Lord any more. Someone has said that God is still waiting to show what He can do for anyone who dares to trust Him all the way. Let me say this to some of you anxious worriers, who worry the way you do because you cannot trust Him: You have trusted God for eternity, but you cannot trust Him for this week, or this day. Then, like Abram, you go down in the pit of despair.

Sins of Believers

Abram "went down." When we do not trust God, we also go down. As a result of Abram's failure to trust God, he does one of the lowest, most despicable, meanest things we find recorded anywhere in the Bible. One sin always leads to another. The record in Genesis 12:11-13 reads as follows.

> And it came to pass, when he was come near to enter into Egypt, that he said unto Sarai his wife, Behold now, I know that thou art a fair woman to look upon:
>
> Therefore it shall come to pass, when the Egyptians shall see thee, that they shall say, This is his wife: and they will kill me, but they will save thee alive.
>
> Say, I pray thee, thou art my sister: that it may be well with me for thy sake; and my soul shall live because of thee.

Here we have an incident that is tremendous in its lesson. A believer who is out of fellowship with God can do meaner and lower things than the sinner who has never been saved. That happens to be the experience of many of us, and we know that it is absolutely true. When we become saved we are new creatures, but God does not repair the "old man," or do a thing to it. He does not even try to repair it, because that which is "born of the flesh is flesh" and will never be any different. He lets others try it. We have the evidence here that Abram in a moment of doubt showed that the old nature and the old doubts were still present within him: he went down into Egypt. Other Biblical characters had similar experiences. We have but to recall the case of Noah and his drunkenness, David and his sin, Solomon and his wives, Peter and his denial of our Lord. "Let him that thinketh he standeth take heed lest he fall."

All these things were written for our admonition and for our instruction. The record of Abram is placed here in order that we may profit by his experience. May the Lord bless to our hearts the lessons from the life of this saint of God. May we profit by his experiences, grow in the grace and in the knowledge of the Lord Jesus Christ, and not make the same mistakes that Abram or the other saints of God have made.

Only trust Him.

CHAPTER SIX

Flesh and Spirit

> And Lot also, which went with Abram, had flocks, and herds, and tents.
>
> And the land was not able to bear them, that they might dwell together: for their substance was great, so that they could not dwell together.
>
> And there was a strife between the herdmen of Abram's cattle and the herdmen of Lot's cattle: and the Canaanite and the Perizzite dwelled then in the land.
>
> And Abram said unto Lot, Let there be no strife, I pray thee, between me and thee, and between my herdmen and thy herdmen; for we be brethren (Genesis 13:5-8).

"Whatsoever a man soweth, that shall he also reap." Those words spoken by Paul apply not only to the sinner, but to the believer in particular. The fact that we are saved and are God's people does not mean that we will not suffer for our mistakes and pay the price for our disobedience. God will and God does judge His people. The believer should not sin, but the fact is that he too often does sin. Not in vain, therefore, does John say in I John 1:8:

> If we say that we have no sin, we deceive ourselves, and the truth is not in us.

And again in verse 10:

> If we say that we have not sinned, we make him a liar, and his word is not in us.

These words were addressed to believers, and John includes himself when he says, "If *we* say that *we* have no sin, *we* deceive ourselves." And yet the believer ought never to sin, for John also says in I John 2:1:

> My little children, these things write I unto you, that ye
> sin not.

The very fact that we are so prone to sin should put us
on our guard against that very possibility. But in spite of
the fact that we ought not to sin, we all too often do. If we
are honest, we will have to admit this. Our Lord knew
beforehand that we would sin after we had been saved, so He
made provision for those sins. He says in I John 1:9:

> If we confess our sins, he is faithful and just to forgive us our
> sins, and to cleanse us from all unrighteousness.

And again in I John 2:1, 2:

> And if any man sin, we have an advocate with the Father,
> Jesus Christ the righteous:
> And he is the propitiation for our sins: and not for
> ours only, but also for the sins of the whole world.

How grateful, therefore, we should be that our Saviour, knowing beforehand our weakness and that we would fail after
we were saved, made provision for our forgiveness and
cleansing.

Presumptuous Sinning

Some have corrupted this precious, blessed truth, and made
it the occasion for license and carelessness and looseness of
living. They say that if we sin the Lord is ready to forgive;
we can just ask Him to forgive us and it will be all right
again. They claim therefore, that they can sin again and again
and just be forgiven over again and again. But the Bible
teaches no such thing. While it is true that the Lord forgives
and cleanses us as often as we confess, there is a penalty attached; for even though He forgives, we must still pay the
price. "Whatsoever a man soweth, that shall he also reap" was
written concerning believers. When a Christian disobeys God,
he must pay the price. No Christian can disobey God without reaping the harvest of his disobedience, even though
God freely forgives him.

Abram's Example

Nowhere is this better illustrated than in the life of
Abram, the father of the faithful. God had told him to go
out from the land of his fathers, to another land. This was
the call of faith. Abram believed it, left his country and went
to the land of Canaan. But while he was a believer, he was a
disobedient believer; for instead of leaving his father and his
kindred, he took them along. You will recall the sorrow that
this disobedience brought into Abram's life. God stopped him
half way to Canaan, at Haran, where he spent six barren,
fruitless, miserable years, until he was compelled to bury his
father, a type of the flesh. His disobedience ended in a funeral
far from home. Abram reaped in the death of Terah the sow-
ing of his disobedience of not leaving his father behind
according to the word of God.

Same Lesson Again

In the case of Abram and Lot we have the same experience
graphically repeated. God had said, "Get thee out of thy
country, and from thy *kindred*"; but instead, Abram took Lot
along. God must discipline Abram again for his disobedience.
Lot became a source of grief and sorrow during all the life
of this man of God. After Abram went down into Egypt,
because he, a believer, would not trust his God for the material
things of life, he only laid himself open to still more and
greater sorrow. He took something back from Egypt which
would bring untold trouble into his life. No believer can back-
slide or disobey and be the same again afterwards. He becomes a "crippled priest." He limits his Christian growth and
stunts his life of faith.

Now, we would call your attention to the cattle which
Abram evidently brought with him from Egypt and which
he did not have before.

First Mention

In Genesis 13:2 we read:

And Abram was very rich in cattle, in silver, and in gold.

Now this is the very first mention of cattle in the life of Abram. Before Abram had gone into Egypt he was a shepherd; he returns a cattleman, and these cattle became the occasion for the sad story of the strife betwen Abram and his nephew Lot recorded in this chapter. Notice that the strife was not between Abram's shepherds and Lot's shepherds. Twice we are definitely reminded that it was strife among the *herdmen* and the cattlemen of Abram and Lot. Now this is a very significant statement. Before Abram went to Egypt there is no mention of cattle; now after his backsliding, he has gone into the cattle business.

What bearing, you may ask, has this on the strife between Abram and Lot? It has everything to do with this battle; for sheep can graze and forage where cattle would starve to death. Sheep crop the grass; cows graze. Sheep have teeth in both the upper and the lower jaws; cattle have teeth only in the lower jaw, the front upper jaws being absolutely toothless. As a result, sheep can crop the grass right down to the ground, to the very roots, but cows can only graze where the grass is long enough for them to grasp it with their tongues and to cut it off by holding it against their lower jaw and moving the head upward. Moreover, sheep are noted for eating almost anything — weeds, twigs, branches — and browsing on trees as well as grazing on grass. Hence, land able to support an abundance of sheep may be wholly unable to support an equivalent amount of cattle. This will explain, then, the fact that while the land was able to bear both Abram and Lot's shepherds, it could not begin to bear the cattle they had brought down from Egypt, the type of the world.

Out of Egypt, But —

Abram had left Egypt, but Egypt had not left Abram. Egypt's cattle went with him, and became the occasion for the strife between the brethren before the eyes of the unbelieving Canaanites and Perizzites. How sad, this strife between the brethren; and all of it because of the disobedience on the part of Abram. Had he only trusted God when the famine came, and remained in the land of fellowship, the quarreling would never have happened. Abram is reaping now what he had sown. God did forgive, to be sure, but the penalty had to be borne.

What a warning and lesson all of this presents to us. Believers cannot disobey God and expect to go unpunished and unjudged. They cannot go into the world, and remain unaffected and untainted. To make God's forgiving grace the occasion for careless living is to invite the chastening and the judgment of Almighty God. O, how we wish that we could drive this truth home. Thousands of God's dear children pay until their very dying day for their mistakes and their carelessness in life. Yes, God does forgive, we praise Him for that, but they still pay, pay in remorse, in hindered testimony and in the consciousness of loss of reward and limitations of their joy.

But God Overrules

There is another great lesson here. God could use Abram's mistakes and Abram's sin of backsliding into Egypt the means of separating him from Lot. God had said, "Get thee out . . . from thy kindred," — Lot, who represented the world and Terah, who was a type of the flesh. By a painful experience Abram had gained victory over the flesh when he buried Terah, in Haran. Now he must be separated from the world as well. God in His infinite wisdom can use our failures, yes, even our sin, that He may the better exhibit His grace and make even the wrath of men to praise Him. He, therefore, permitted Abram to disobey; and He used that very disobedience of Abram to carry out His divine plan to separate Abram from the world in the process of perfecting his faith. Of course, Abram was in no wise justified in his disobedience, but God could still overrule to accomplish His purpose in Abram's life in preparation for the final victory of faith when he withheld not his own son, Isaac. Without these experiences both of failure and of success, defeat and victory, Abram could never have attained the glorious climax of his faith whereby he earned the distinction of being called the "father of the faithful" and the "friend of God." Yes, where sin did abound, grace did much more abound.

ABRAM LEARNED A LESSON

Through Abram's backsliding and God's chastening of his sin, Abram learned an important lesson. He never went back to Egypt again, and instead of rebelling against the sad result of his sin, he acknowledged his guilt. He proved that he had learned a tremendous lesson by magnanimously settling the strife. His conduct is evidence of his growth in grace, even through the experience of failure and sorrow. Listen to him now in Genesis 13:8:

> And Abram said unto Lot, Let there be no strife, I pray thee, between me and thee, and between my herdmen and thy herdmen; for we be brethren.
>
> Is not the whole land before thee? separate thyself, I pray thee, from me: if thou wilt take the left hand, then I will go to the right; or if thou depart to the right hand, then I will go to the left (Genesis 13:8-9).

He says to Lot, in effect, "Lot, I am willing to be the least; I am willing to take the loss if need be, I will let you take the very best; You may take your choice." Now Abram had every right in the world to demand just exactly the opposite. He had been called to Canaan, not Lot. God had given the land to Abram, not to his nephew. God had made His covenant with Abram, and not with Lot who had come along as a hanger-on. Abram was the eldest of the two, and could expect Lot to recognize this important fact. Yet Abram did nothing of the kind. Instead, he did the very opposite.

WHY THIS GRACIOUSNESS

The reason for this magnanimous graciousness on the part of Abram and his conduct toward Lot we have already seen. First of all, Abram believed God's Word that He would take care of him no matter what the immediate sacrifice might be, and would ultimately give him the land which He had promised to him. This was the triumph of Abram's faith. But I think there is another reason suggested in the text here which is very important. We read, for instance, in verse 7 that "the Canaanite and the Perizzite were then in the land." There must be reason, since we believe in verbal inspiration, why the Holy Spirit caused Moses to insert this particular sentence in the record here. It is, indeed, very suggestive. Here were two brethren, Abram and Lot, who claimed to be worshippers of the one true Jehovah, and claimed to be men of faith; yet they were fighting and quibbling and striving with each other, and in that way were losing their testimony. There can be no reason to doubt that the Canaanites and the Perizzites were looking at Abram and Lot critically and wondering whether there would be any evidence of the reality of the faith which they both professed to have. Abram, recognizing this fact, was willing to be the least, and for the time being take a definite loss in order that his testimony might not be hindered, the name of the Lord might not be smirched, and no reproach brought upon the cause of the One in whom He claimed to trust.

This portion of Abraham's history certainly holds a tremendous lesson for us in these days of sectarianism and separation among believers. Today too, the Canaanite and the Perizzite are still in the land and are looking critically and scrutinously at all those who profess to be followers of the Lord Jesus Christ. Certainly the quibbling and the dissension and the division and the fighting among believers is construed by them as an evidence that we are not what we profess to be. May the Lord teach us from the lesson of Abram to have more charity, to be willing to be the least, and for conscience's sake to take loss if need be, in order that the Lord Jesus may truly be exalted; "for none of us liveth to himself, and no man dieth to himself" (Romans 14:7).

CHAPTER SEVEN

The Lust of the Eye

> And Lot lifted up his eyes, and beheld all the plain of Jordan, that it was well watered every where, before the Lord destroyed Sodom and Gomorrah, even as the garden of the Lord, like the land of Egypt, as thou comest unto Zoar.
>
> Then Lot chose him all the plain of Jordan; and Lot journeyed east: and they separated themselves the one from the other (Genesis 13:10, 11).
>
> But the men of Sodom were wicked and sinners before the Lord exceedingly (vs. 13).

The story of the separation of two brethren because of sins which had been committed in their lives previously is a sad one. Lot, the nephew of Abram, had never learned to walk by faith, but only by sight. His actions were entirely controlled by what he saw, not by what He heard the word of the Lord say. In II Corinthians 5:7 we read:

> We walk by faith, and not by sight.

The Lord expects the believer to walk by faith and the promises of God alone. This is what makes Abraham the great example of faith; for we are told of him in Hebrews 11:8:

> By faith Abraham, when he was called to go out into a place which he should after receive for an inheritance, obeyed; and he went out, *not knowing whither he went.*

When God called Abram, He did not show him where he was going at all. Abram was supposed to go in faith, without sight. God speaks to us and expects us to believe Him upon the testimony of His word without any additional evidence, if need be, except the hearing of faith. How different it is with the natural man. The natural man wants to see instead of believe. God says "faith is the evidence of things not seen," but man says sight is the evidence — "seeing is believing." This last phrase is the slogan of the world.

The difference between these two ways is illustrated in a most striking way in the history of Abram and Lot. Abram heard God's word, believed it and acted upon it. Lot wanted to see instead. We read of him that he "lifted up his eyes, and beheld all the plain of Jordan . . . Then Lot chose him all the plain of Jordan." God's Word says to us, "incline thine ear and hear," but Lot closed his ears, and opened his eyes instead. This was the great mistake in the life of Lot. He chose wicked Sodom, on the evidence of what his eyes beheld. Abram had made his choice on the basis of faith in what God had said. Lot made his choice by sight, and ended in disaster, while Abram's choice of faith ended in victory.

We are endowed normally with five senses: feeling, smelling, tasting, hearing and seeing. Through these five senses we receive all of our physical and mental impressions, but it is through two of these particularly, seeing and hearing, that we receive by far the greatest bulk of these impressions. We are influenced in our moral and spiritual life almost entirely by what we hear and by what we see, rather than by what we feel, taste and smell. The two wide gates to the soul of man are the ear and the eye.

FAITH COMETH BY HEARING

Now the ear is the channel through which God speaks to man, while Satan's approach seems usually to be through the eye of man. The ear is the portal of faith, while the eye is often the gateway for evil. The experience of Lot when he substituted sight for faith, the eye for the ear, and chose Sodom by sight, is not the only evidence in the Bible that the ear is the organ through which the Lord speaks while the eye is peculiarly the organ of entry for the Devil himself. Paul tells us distinctly in Romans 10:17:

52

> So then faith cometh by hearing, and hearing by the word
> of God.

Faith cometh by hearing, the hearing of the Word, and not
by the seeing with the eye.

We might fill a volume to show from the Word of God
and from actual experience that the eye is the peculiar organ
through which Satan most frequently tempts men, and causes
them to fall. We have but to go to the very first temptation in
human history, recorded in Genesis 2:16, 17:

> Of every tree of the garden thou mayest freely eat:
> But of the tree of the knowledge of good and evil, thou
> shalt not eat of it: for in the day that thou eatest thereof thou
> shalt surely die.

This is what God *said* to Adam as He placed him in the
Garden. But now notice how the Devil came. He said, "Eve,
you are missing something by just listening to God's Word.
He is holding back something that He does not want you to
see." Therefore he said:

> For God doth know that in the day ye eat thereof, then
> *your eyes shall be opened* (Genesis 3:5).

The Devil promised to show Eve something. He said, "You'll
see something you haven't seen before." God had said, "Believe My Word," but the Devil came and said, "See and
find out for yourself." We read the dire result in Genesis
3:6:

> And when the woman *saw* that the tree was good for food
> . . . she took of the fruit thereof.

Until the time when Eve *saw* the fruit of the tree, she had
successfully resisted Satan; but when she *saw*, when Satan's
attack came through the eye, she fell. We know the tragic
result.

Look for a moment at the case of Achan in Joshua 7, which
resulted in the defeat of the armies of Israel before Ai. Here
is Achan's confession, recorded in verse 21:

> When I *saw* among the spoils a goodly Babylonish garment
> . . . then I coveted them, and took them.

Again it all began when Achan coveted with his eyes the things of which God had said, "Destroy everything." Achan disregarded what God had *said*, and what he had heard; rather was he influenced by what he *saw*.

Jesus also recognized the fact that Satan's temptation came largely through the eye when He tells us, "If thine eye be single, thy whole body shall be full of light." In the three-fold temptation of Jesus, all these temptations were originally through the eye. Satan showed Him the stones and challenged Him to turn them into bread in the desert, saying: "Command these stones to be turned to bread." Again it was through the eye when he took Him up to the pinnacle of the temple where He could look all about Him on the city of Jerusalem. Then again from a high mountain, in the third temptation, he showed Him all the kingdoms of the world and their glory. But Jesus met Satan's temptation to the eye by quoting what God had *said*.

Dangerous Appeal to the Eye

In this present age of illustrations, images and pictures — still and moving, good and bad — the events just cited should make us ponder seriously. Can we not link the rapid decline in morals, the awful increase in crime and murder and violence, to the tremendous emphasis placed on pictures and the appeal to the eye, instead of to the ear of man. In the second commandment there is more than appears on the surface when God said, "Thou shalt not make thee any graven image, or any likeness of anything that is in heaven above, or that is in the earth beneath, or that is in the waters beneath the earth" (Deuteronomy 5:8). Surely here is at least a suggestion already of the tremendous danger which lurks in the things that we *see* instead of those we hear. It is significant that the Bible is not an illustrated book. There are no pictures of any kind in the Bible, and we personally often feel that it is wrong and sacrilegious to insert pictures in the book which God himself left wholly without illustrations. It is a sign of the times that man refuses to hear and listen to God. Man is too busy looking at the things the Devil has prepared for the eye.

Our age is truly the illustrated, the picture age. Everything we do must be illustrated. Everything we advertise must be accompanied by pictures, from beer to soda crackers, and usually with pictures at least suggestive, if not bordering on the obscene. On our billboards, in our magazines, on every page of the newspaper, the appeal is to the eye through the pictures that are there set forth. Many of the illustrations in the average news sheet, not only on the theatre page, but on almost every page, should make one blush for shame.

What page does the family fight about the most? It is always the funnies. Our children go mad over comic books. The array of magazine covers displayed in the literature departments of many of our establishments, drug stores, grocery stores, not even to mention the lewd contraband publications distributed more or less secretly and underground, are a curse and disgrace to a decent community. I remind you again, therefore, that when Eve *saw* that the tree was good for food, when Lot *saw* that the plain of Jordan was well watered, when Achan *saw* a goodly Babylonish garment, that then they began their downward journey.

IN THE CHURCH

Today the enemy has invaded even the sacred precincts of the church of the living God. When I was a child no pictures were ever shown in the church. It was exclusively a place of worship, for prayer, for praise, for reverence and for the hearing of the "thus saith the Lord." The Word occupied the most prominent place in the service; the sermons were often an hour long. Then gradually the appeal to the eye crept in. First there were harmless stereopticons of a moral, religious or cultural nature. Then came the motion pictures. Today in many churches, entertainment has largely replaced prayer; pictures have replaced the preaching of the Word of God; and hundreds of preachers have succumbed to Lot's temptation, because they have found that pictures will get a bigger crowd and a better offering than the simple, plain "thus saith the Lord." Many a church cannot get a baker's dozen out to a prayer meeting or to a preaching service, but it can pack the house with a "sanctified" show, or a western movie in a religious garb, or a minstrel show.

Add to all this the introduction of television, with its tremendous potentialities for evil if not strictly controlled, and we have, we believe, the answer to the question, What is the cause of the tremendous increase in crime, especially juvenile crime, immorality, wickedness and irresponsibility, and the breakdown of the home? It was Satan's master stroke when he showed Eve the tree, when he caused Lot to behold the plain of Jordan, and Achan the Babylonish garment. When Eve's eyes were opened by sin, her ears were immediately closed to the voice of God. The more the appeal is made today through the eye, beautiful as the programs may be, the less people will care for the Word of God.

HINDRANCE, NOT AID TO FAITH

Now, of course, I hear objection made constantly to this sort of reasoning by people who say that pictures, images, icons and all the rest, are an aid to our faith. They help us to visualize what God has already said in His Word. This, beloved, will not, we personally believe, stand the test of Scripture. If God had wanted it thus, and if these things were such a great and necessary aid to faith, He certainly would not have waited centuries and centuries before He permitted man to discover them. It is our firm, personal opinion that God wants us to believe His Word without any other evidence or aid, and that all these so-called aids to faith are rather hindrances and a clever ruse of Satan to draw us away from the Word of the living God.

That is why we preach, that is why we broadcast and teach the Word of God, instead of touring the country presenting religious entertainments and sanctified vaudeville. It is with

gravest concern that we view the rapidly increasing tendency to
crowd the teaching and the preaching of the Word of God
more and more into the background in our services and relegate
it to a subordinate and unimportant place in many of our
meetings. Instead of the Word being the all-important thing,
the tendency is to limit it to a brief sermonette, often superficial, shallow and frothy, while most of the time in the service is given over to interminable, wearisome preliminaries,
non-essentials and often mere entertainment. The result can be
nothing else than a coming generation of frivolous, shallow,
superficial Christians who will fall before the first onslaught
of the enemy because they do not have the foundation of the
Word under their feet. Lot walked by sight, not by faith.
We fear the days of Sodom are being repeated with all the
appeal to the eye, accompanied by neglect of the Word of
God. It is not in vain that the Lord has said:

> As it was in the days of Lot . . . Even thus shall it be in
> the day when the Son of man is revealed (Luke 17:28, 30).

What to Do

Now, of course, the question arises, What are we going to
do about it? Listen, beloved, if you share our fears and our mis-
givings in this matter, you can do one thing: voice your ve-
hement disapproval and insist on more of the Word of God
and less of the appeal to the flesh in your own church and
in your own services. You can carefully supervise the things
which your children are allowed to see and look at in the
home. It can be done if you start early enough and have
courage to be firm enough. You can pray for a revival of
interest in the Word of God and the teaching of the Word
of God among believers.

CHAPTER EIGHT

Abraham the Intercessor

. . . but Abraham stood yet before the Lord (Genesis 18:22).

Faith which is never tested will never grow strong. Faith must be exercised or it will ever be weak. This is the reason God permits the trials and the temptations which characterize the life of every believer and test his faith, sometimes to the very limit of endurance. Steel must be tempered with fire to become keen. A tree must face storms in order to become strong and be pruned if it is to bring forth fruit. Gold cannot be purified without passing through the fire. Silver must be constantly polished to remain bright. The soil must be plowed and broken and crushed before it can bring forth friut. Even so, the believer needs to be constantly tried and tested if he is to grow in faith and become a fruitful Christian.

For whom the Lord loveth he chasteneth, and scourgeth every son whom he receiveth (Hebrews 12:6).

NORMAL EXPERIENCE

This is the law of the Christian life. God is constantly testing and trying us, passing us through the fire and under the rod, that out of each testing and each trial we may emerge stronger, purer and better able to meet the next and possibly even greater trial, until at the last we shall reach the stature of perfection when we see Him face to face. The Christian who experiences no trials or tribulations, who endures no chastening, may well seriously question his fellowship with Christ. Our Lord Himself has said:

> In the world ye shall have tribulation: but be of good cheer;
> I have overcome the world (John 16:33).

And the Apostle Peter tells us this:

> That the trial of your faith, being much more precious
> than of gold that perisheth, though it be tried with fire, might
> be found unto praise and honour and glory at the appearing of
> Jesus Christ (I Peter 1:7).

It is the normal experience of the believer, and not the abnormal, to be tested and tried and purified.

God has however, promised to give the grace, the supply for each trial, so that we may profit by each test and receive strength for the next trial to come. The Holy Spirit Himself has assured us:

> There hath no temptation taken you but such as is common
> to man: but God is faithful, who will not suffer you to be
> tempted above that ye are able; but will with the temptation
> also make a way to escape, that ye may be able to bear it
> (I Corinthians 10:13).

Instead of fainting, therefore, and becoming discouraged when trials and temptations beset us, we should rejoice to know that God is still dealing with us as children. We should the rather ask the question, Just what is our Father trying to teach us now and do with us? What is the lesson of trust and faith that He would have us learn through these trying experiences?

The life of Abraham then becomes a wonderful example, and for this reason he is called "the father of the faithful." His life presents a series of testings and trials, successes and failures, but even the failures are used of God to lift him to a higher plane of faith and prepare him to meet still greater tests of faith, until they reach their climax in Genesis 22 at the offering of his only son, Isaac, by faith in the promises of God.

SPEAKING BOLDLY

After each test Abraham's faith becomes stronger. In Genesis 18 we have wonderful evidence of this fact. Here Abraham becomes the great prevailing intercessor for his backslidden nephew, Lot. The wickedness of Sodom and Gomorrah had reached its peak, and God determines to destroy these wicked cities. Before He does, the Lord informs Abraham of His intentions. How wonderful to know that we can be on such good terms with Almighty God that He is willing to take us into His confidence and inform us beforehand of His plans. We read in Genesis 18:17:

> Shall I hide from Abraham that thing which I do.

God is ready now to destroy the wicked cities, and Abraham immediately begins to intercede in behalf of the city, for the sake of the righteous who are dwelling therein. We suggest that you read very carefully Genesis 18:23-33. In these verses we have a marvelous picture of Abraham, the intercessor. He has now grown so far in the life of faith that he dares to stand alone between God and the doomed cities to hold back the judgment of the Almighty. Abraham says to the Lord boldly:

> Peradventure there be fifty righteous within the city: wilt thou also destroy and not spare the place for the fifty righteous that are therein? (Genesis 18:24).

And God answers him:

> If I find in Sodom fifty righteous within the city, then I will spare all the place for their sakes (Genesis 18:26).

Abraham then becomes bolder, and reduces the number of the righteous in Sodom to forty-five, then thirty, then twenty, and finally to ten, and says:

> Peradventure ten shall be found there (Genesis 18:32).

And again God answers him and says:

> I will not destroy it for ten's sake (Genesis 18:32).

MOST IMPORTANT PEOPLE

Many important lessons lie here in the story of Abraham, the intercessor. First is the importance of believers in the world. The most important people in all the world are that little company of often unrecognized but indispensable, born-again believers, who are walking apart from the world in fellowship with their Lord. So important are the believers in Christ that God will not bring judgment upon this old, wicked world until He has informed them concerning it. So important is the true Church of Jesus Christ that it can stand between God and judgment and prevail upon God to stay His hand in mercy. It was so with Abraham. He held back the destruction of Sodom by his own intercession.

Lot, too, was a believer and a righteous man, but he was a carnal, backslidden man, out of fellowship and walking after the flesh. Although a believer, he had no power with God and no testimony. It was due to Abraham's intercession, not Lot's worth, that the city was spared until Lot was safely out. It is of most impressive significance, therefore, that Jesus, when speaking of the last days just before His coming again, compares those days to the days before the doom of Sodom. He says, "As it was in the days of Lot . . . Even thus shall it be in the day when the Son of man is revealed" (Luke 17:28, 30).

Sodom was spared for a time because one man walking with God, interceded and stood in the gap. God did not finally destroy the city until Lot was safely out. Here, indeed, is a marvelous lesson for these days when we hear so much about revival. One man, Abraham, interceding with God, kept back the hand of judgment.

The case is no different today. Remember Jesus' words, "As it was in the days of Lot . . . Even thus shall it be in the day when the Son of man is revealed." The sins of Sodom are being repeated today with a vengeance. The wickedness, the immorality, dishonesty, graft, violence, ungodliness of the world seem to surpass even the days of Sodom. Professing Christendom, like Lot, is utterly blinded to the impending doom. It is wholly unaware that God's hand is even now raised this very moment to bring judgment upon the earth and upon our fair nation. It continues to prate about a better world, winning the world for Christ, bringing in the kingdom without the coming of the King Himself.

STANDING IN THE GAP

The world and professing Christendom are unaware that the only reason the hell of God's judgment has not yet fallen upon the nations is that there is in this world today a company, a small, despised company of believers who like Abraham, walking in fellowship with the Lord, are holding back God's awful judgment. This little company receives but scant notice in the world. It is mostly disregarded and receives little publicity in the newspapers. It is often considered extremist and fanatic because it preaches judgment and the imminent coming of the Lord to judge the world. This small company, however, still contains the most important people in all of the world's affairs today.

SALT OF THE EARTH

Jesus said of this company of believers, "Ye are the salt of of the earth" (Matthew 5:13). Yes, indeed, God's people are the salt of the earth. Salt retards corruption. Salt will not prevent corruption from setting in eventually, but it retards it and delays it. So, too, the presence in the world today of a company of believers called "the salt of the earth" is the only reason God has not yet visited this world with catastrophe and judgment. Man is frantic in his fear of world catastrophe in this atomic age with all sorts of strange signs in the heavens. He has set up organizations and committees and associations and alliances; he has spent billions for defense, and signed pacts and agreements in an effort to avert the atomic end of the world. But more important, yes, all important in holding back the judgment of God is this other company, this little company, the "salt of the earth."

NEEDS BUT LITTLE

It does not take a great deal of salt to flavor and to preserve, usually only a pinch. So, too, a few believers, yes, one believer, has more power with God than a world full of diplomats and statesmen. This truly gives us a thrill. Sometimes we feel a bit neglected and lonely in this world when we realize how the world gives us so little recognition; but after all, we are exceedingly important by the grace of God. We are so important in fact, that even the devil cannot do what he wants to do in this old world because of our presence here below. Yes, indeed, the Lord says of us, we are "the salt of the earth."

The Bible abounds with examples of the power of intercession of believers. Of course, Abraham is the great example here, but we remember also Moses who was able to hold back the hand of God by his intercession in behalf of Israel. After Israel's great sin of making the golden calf we hear God saying:

> Let me alone, that my wrath may wax hot against them, and that I may consume them: and I will make of thee a great nation (Exodus 32:10).

"Let Me alone," says the Almighty to a puny man like Moses, "Let Me alone." It is as though God were saying: "You are hindering Me and preventing Me from sending judgment upon this wicked, backslidden nation." What a tremendous testimony that one man, Moses, interceding for Israel could prevail with God; for Moses does cry out, "Oh, spare them for Thy mercy's sake," and in Psalm 106:23 we read this:

> Therefore he [God] said that he would destroy them [Israel] had not Moses his chosen stood before him in the breach, to turn away his wrath, lest he should destroy them.

Moses was indeed, the salt of the earth in those days. When finally God did come to judge Israel, it was because the salt had lost its power and there was found no intercessor. In Ezekiel 22:30 we read these tremendously significant words:

> And I sought for a man among them, that should make up the hedge, and stand in the gap before me for the land, that I should not destroy it: but I found none.

> Therefore have I poured out mine indignation upon them; I have consumed them with the fire of my wrath.

God virtually says, "I would not have come to destroy Israel if

I could have found a man to intercede, to stand in the gap;
who, like Abraham and Moses, would avert destruction and
stay the hand of my judgment."

Christians, we are the ones who retard and are able to
hold back the judgment of God and prevent this world from
being destroyed at man's own hand. It is not only our presence
as the salt in the world, but our intercession, our prayers,
which are wielding the powers which restrain the hand of
God. Without Christians standing in the gap, all the efforts of
men and nations must and will fail. I appeal to you as
Christians to realize the important position which you hold
here below. The destiny of our blessed land is in our power
far more than in the hands of diplomats, statesmen and inter-
national politicians. Let us, therefore, rededicate our lives to
a service of prayer and intercession for our land and for the
upholding of the Word of God, of prayer for our rulers, our
government and our authorities; and let us practice Paul's
admonition:

> That, first of all, supplications, prayers, intercessions, and
> giving of thanks, be made for all men;
>
> For kings, and for all that are in authority; that we may lead
> a quiet and peaceable life in all godliness and honesty.
>
> For this is good and acceptable in the sight of God our
> Saviour (I Timothy 2:1-3).

Ye are the salt of the earth.

CHAPTER NINE

The Rapture in Genesis

Haste thee, escape thither; for I cannot do any thing till thou be come thither (Genesis 19:22).

These words were spoken to a worldly, carnal man of God by the name of Lot, just before God destroyed Sodom and Gomorrah. They are probably the most remarkable words in this great nineteenth chapter of Genesis which records the second greatest catastrophe in the history of man upon the earth. The presence today of the great Dead Sea in Palestine and its surrounding deserts stands as an eternal testimony of the extent and severity of this tremendous stroke of God's judgment upon the wicked cities of the plain of Palestine.

God had determined to destroy the wicked cities with fire from heaven and had already informed Abraham, His faithful friend, about it. God delayed His actions and withheld His hand of judgment because of Abraham's prayer, but now the time is come. However, God will not bring the fire of destruction upon the city until one single family has first been taken out of Sodom. As long as Lot is there, God has promised that He will not, cannot send the fire from heaven. That is the force of the words of our text.

We must remember that Lot was a believer; he was a righteous man, though worldly, carnal, fleshly and entirely out of fellowship with His Lord. That Lot was a believer is without a single question in the light of II Peter 2:7 and 8, where Peter tells us that God delivered just Lot, vexed with the filthy conversation of the wicked:

(For that righteous man dwelling among them, in seeing and hearing, vexed his righteous soul from day to day with their unlawful deeds).

Lot, then, was a worldly believer, not walking in fellowship with the Lord. But he was still a believer; and God said, as it were, "Even though you were unfaithful, Lot, I am going to be faithful"; for if we are unfaithful, yet "he abideth faithful: he cannot deny himself" (II Timothy 2:13).

This account, however, goes far deeper than only revealing God's faithfulness to an erring child. Very true, Lot was saved, even though he had built only hay, wood and stubble; for God has said: "If any man's work shall be burned, he shall suffer loss: but he himself shall be saved; yet so as by fire" (I Corinthians 3:15). But our Lord Jesus Christ uses this incident for a much broader lesson. Speaking of His second coming — a time when He will judge the world for its iniquity by sending the great tribulation of which the destruction of Sodom is only a type — our Saviour tells us definitely:

And as it was in the days of Noe, so shall it be also in the days of the Son of man (Luke 17:26).

Likewise also as it was in the days of Lot; they did eat, they drank, they bought, they sold, they planted, they builded;

But the same day that Lot went out of Sodom it rained fire and brimstone from heaven, and destroyed them all.

Even thus shall it be in the day when the Son of man is revealed (Luke 17:28-30).

The teaching here, of course, is unmistakable. God would not destroy Sodom until Lot was safely out. And, therefore, He says: "Haste thee, escape thither; for I cannot do any thing till thou be come thither." But just as soon as Noah was safe in the ark, and just as soon as Lot was out of Sodom, the judgment of God fell without any delay.

These are the two historical incidents in the history of man, and the only two, which Jesus used to portray conditions as they will be at the end of the age and at His coming again. Countless are the lessons and suggestions here, but we are particularly interested now in the application definitely taught here by Jesus concerning *who* will be taken out at the rapture at Jesus' coming. The two incidents of Noah and Lot should settle the question forever, if there were nothing else in the Bible.

Two Kinds of Believers

We face the question squarely: Who will be raptured at Jesus' coming, which we believe to be imminent? Some tell us that the Church will have to pass through the tribulation. This is called the post-tribulation rapture. Then there are others who say that the Church will pass through only a part of the tribulation, and will be raptured somewhere in the middle of that awful day. This has been called the mid-tribulation rapture. Still others there are who say that only the sanctified believers, those who have had a second blessing and a second work of grace, will be raptured; all the rest, the carnal believers, will have to pass through the tribulation period to be purified. These we call partial rapture-ists. Now the teaching of the Lord Jesus concerning Noah and Lot brands every one of these theories as an unscriptural error, and we shall seek to show this to you from the Word of God.

Remember that Noah and Lot were both saved out of the judgment before it fell. Noah was a spiritual believer who walked with God and was safely hid in the ark in comfort and in peace. Lot was a carnal, worldly believer, out of fellowship with his Lord, but he too was taken out before the judgment fell. There was, of course, a vast difference, as we shall see, in *how* they were saved, but both escaped the judgment and condemnation which fell upon the earth.

Remember, too, that the flood and the destruction of Sodom are pictures of the judgment of God at the return of the Lord Jesus Christ according to our Lord's own words. They are types of the tribulation. If the words of the Lord Jesus concerning Noah and Lot mean anything whatsoever, they mean that *all* believers will be caught away before the tribulation starts. Lot, the worldly believer, was taken out before, as well as Noah, the spiritual believer. How anyone with an open Bible before him can in the face of this clear revelation teach that the Church must pass through all or part of the tribulation only illustrates how our enemy even deceives the children of God, and seeks to rob them of that blessed hope of the rapture of the saints before the judgment of God falls upon this wicked earth.

What a Difference

While the Bible teaches beyond a question of a doubt the rapture of all saints before the tribulation, it also shows that there will be different results. In I Corinthians 3 we have two classes of believers sharply separated, who will appear at the judgment seat of Christ immediately following the rapture of the saints. Some who built upon the Rock, gold, silver and precious stones will receive a reward and commendation; others who built only hay, wood and stubble will *suffer* loss. They will lose everything but eternal life, and be saved so as by fire.

Peter tells us in II Peter 1:11 that if we give diligence to make our calling and election sure that then:

> an entrance shall be ministered unto you abundantly into the everlasting kingdom of our Lord and Saviour Jesus Christ.

There is according to this passage "an abundant entrance," implying that there will also be an entrance by "the skin of the teeth."

In I John 2:28 we read this:

> And now, little children, abide in him; that, when he shall appear, we may have confidence, and not be ashamed before him at his coming.

Here we have the definite statement that there will be two classes of believers, some who will meet the Lord with con-

fidence when He comes, and others who will be ashamed at
His appearing.

Then again, in II John, verse 8, we read this:

> Look to yourselves, that we lose not those things which we
> have wrought, but that we receive a *full* reward.

Here we have the statement that when the Lord comes there
will be some who will have a full reward, and this, of course,
suggests that there will be some who will not have a full
reward, but will be saved so as by the skin of the teeth. Some
will have confidence, while others will be ashamed at His appearing. Some will receive rewards, while others will suffer
loss and be saved so as by fire.

Surely this is the clear teaching of the Word of God, and
this is the teaching of Noah who was ready to enter the ark
and of Lot who had to be dragged out of Sodom. Noah went
in comfort, with every need supplied in peace and safety.
Lot came out, leaving everything behind, with the smell of
fire and brimstone in his clothes, saved so as by fire. Noah
had the accommodation of a spacious ark with all his saved
family. Lot, the former alderman of Sodom, mighty politician,
who sat in the gate, in the place of authority, lived in a
cave with his two daughters, while his two sons perished in
the fire and his wife became a pillar of salt.

The point is, I trust, clear: the Bible teaches plainly that
all the saints will be raptured before the judgment of the tribulation, but this does not mean that we shall all fare alike when
we appear before the judgment seat of Christ. We cannot live
as we please here below, for God will judge His people. We
suggest that you read carefully the shameful record of Lot
in the cave with his two daughters, and the awful sin which
resulted in these two girls having children by their own father.
Yes, Noah went into the ark with confidence; Lot fled Sodom
with fear and shame. Lot found that mortgages on property
in Sodom were a bad investment, while Abraham looked for

a city that hath foundations, whose builder and whose maker is God.

FURTHER EVIDENCE

Many other passages in Scripture corroborate the great fact that God will not bring judgment upon the earth until the saints of God are first caught away. Speaking of the coming day of the Lord and the tribulation, Paul tells us in II Thessalonians 2:6 and 7:

> And now ye know what withholdeth that he [the man of sin] might be revealed in his time.
>
> For the mystery of iniquity doth already work: only he who now letteth [hindereth] will let, until he be taken out of the way.

The entire structure of Revelation teaches the same thing. In Revelation 2 and 3 we have the history of the Church beginning with the Ephesian church and ending with the Laodicean, and a repetition of the days of Noah and Lot, when Christ is pushed outside the door. In Revelation 6 to 19 we have the tribulation, but before it can begin, John is raptured into heaven. There, representing the Church, he beholds the judgment on earth from his place in heaven. God had said unto Lot, "Haste thee, escape thither; for I cannot do any thing until thou be come thither."

Soon that day foreshadowed by the destruction of Sodom will be here. Everything seems to be ripe for the coming of the Lord, when

> The Lord Himself shall descend from heaven with a shout, with the voice of the archangel, and with the trump of God: and the dead in Christ shall rise first:
>
> Then we which are alive and remain shall be caught up together with them in the clouds, to meet the Lord in the air: and so shall we ever be with the Lord (I Thessalonians 4:16-17).

The question is this, Are you, my friend, ready? Yes, I am addressing Christians. Are you ready? When the shout occurs from heaven, will you like Noah be ready to go when God says, "Come thou and all thy house into the ark?" Or will you, like Lot, have to be torn out and be saved so as by fire? Will you go in with your children because you have trusted God and claimed them for Him, or will you, like Lot, have to leave some of your precious ones behind? The blessed hope is only a blessed hope for those who are ready. For others it will be, as for Lot, a time of shame and regret and tears. They will find their works all burned and they themselves saved so as by fire.

Sinner, while this message is particularly to believers, there is also a word for you. Remember Lot's two sons perished in the fire. Remember Lot's wife. She too was a professing Christian, and made a start as though to leave. She acted as though she belonged to those who would escape the judgment, but when the test came it was revealed that her religion was only a profession and a sham. Remember Lot's wife. You may rely upon your church membership, your profession, but it cannot save you in the end, for Jesus said, "Ye must be born again."

CHAPTER TEN

The Ground of Faith

> What shall we say then that Abraham our father, as pertaining to the flesh, hath found?
>
> For if Abraham were justified by works, he hath whereof to glory; but not before God.
>
> For what saith the scripture? Abraham believed God, and it was counted unto him for righteousness.
>
> Now to him that worketh is the reward not reckoned of grace, but of debt.
>
> But to him that worketh not, but believeth on him that justifieth the ungodly, his faith is counted for righteousness (Romans 4:1-5).

This passage begins with a question which the Apostle Paul anticipated in view of what he had set forth in the preceding three chapters of Romans. He had proven the utter depravity of human nature and the complete helplessness of man in saving himself by his own works and by the keeping of the law. Having done this, Paul declares that salvation is entirely by faith, wholly apart from the works of the law. This was not a welcome truth to the legalists of his day, who prided themselves upon their own goodness and righteousness and boasted of their law-keeping. Paul, therefore, directs their attention to father Abraham, and asks, "How was Abraham saved?" By faith, or by the works of the law? Certainly not by keeping the law, for the law was not given until at least four hundred years after Abraham was born. Paul then appeals to the Scripture itself. That, after all, is the final authority, not man's word, not the teaching of some church, not some man's dogma, not your opinion. Paul quotes from Genesis 15 these words:

> Abraham believed God, and it was counted unto him for righteousness.

It was, then, all by faith, and faith alone, wholly apart from the works of the law. Abraham believed God. Now Paul does not say that Abraham believed *in* God, but rather, he believed *God*. There is a vast difference between believing *in* God, and believing *God*. All men, except fools, believe in God; that is, they believe there is a God; but most of them do not believe a word He says.

GENESIS 15

The question, therefore, immediately arises, What did Abraham believe? What was it that God said, which Abraham believed, and which saved him and was counted to him for righteousness? We have the answer in the chapter from which Paul quotes, Genesis 15. Genesis 15 is the great faith chapter of the Old Testament, just as Hebrews 11 is of the New Testament. In it God reveals His one and only way of salvation. In Genesis 15 God reveals for the first time His complete plan of salvation in all of its fullness. The chapter opens with these significant words:

> After these things the word of the Lord came unto Abram in a vision, saying, Fear not, Abram: I am thy shield, and thy exceeding great reward.

Abram has just returned from his great victory over the four kings of the north, and he has delivered Lot and his family and the five other kings. Now he becomes afraid, and fears that the kings against whom he fought will come back for revenge later on. Moreover, he has refused to take any of the spoil and this too may have troubled him. It is then that the Lord comes to encourage him, and says, "Fear not, Abram: I am thy shield." That is, "Don't be afraid, Abram, for I will be your protector." Then the Lord adds, "and thy exceeding great reward." God seems to say, "You have refused the wealth of the spoils of the king of Sodom, but I myself will be your reward."

We digress from the story long enough here to point out a most arresting fact in this record of Genesis 15. There are a number of words and expressions used for the very first time in the Bible in this particular passage. While these words occur hundreds of times later on, they are never used until in this chapter. These expressions deal with God's plan of justification and so they are never used until this particular chapter which deals with the faith of Abraham. Here are just a few of them:

1. "The Word of the Lord." This expression occurs in verse 1. Although it occurs over and over in the Bible, it is never used until in this particular verse. It sets forth the basic truth of salvation, that justification is always by the Word of the Lord. No one has ever yet been saved, not one will ever be saved, except by God's Word. Peter tells us in I Peter 1:23: "Being born again, not of corruptible seed, but of incorruptible, by the word of God, which liveth and abideth for ever."

2. "Believed." This word occurs in verse 6. It is very remarkable that God never permitted the use of this word, one of the commonest words in the entire Bible, until in this chapter, the faith chapter of the Old Testament. This word emphasizes the fact that salvation is not only by the "Word of God," but by *believing* the Word of God.

3. "Fear not." It also occurs in verse 1. This expression tells us the result of justification by faith. Freedom from fear and peace with God are the result of faith in His promises. Paul tells us in Romans 5:1: "Therefore being justified by faith, we have peace with God through our Lord Jesus Christ."

4. "Reward." This word is in the first verse, too. It reminds us that the reward of faith is justification in the sight of God by the Word of God.

ABRAM'S DESIRE

To return to the narrative: After God has promised to protect Abram and reward him, Abram begins to question God emphatically. He reminds the Lord that he is not primarily interested at all in the things which he had refused from the King of Sodom, but rather in the fulfillment of a promise which God had made many, many years before, and which up until now He had not fulfilled. God had promised Abram a son by Sarah his wife. The years had slipped by, and it was now thirty years since God had promised this son whom Abram desired so much. Abram reminds God of this and says:

> Lord God, what wilt thou give me, seeing I go childless, and the steward of my house is this Eliezer of Damascus?
>
> And Abram said, Behold, to me thou hast given no seed: and, lo, one born in my house is mine heir (Genesis 15:2, 3).

Abram here complains bitterly that the promise of a seed has not been kept. The Lord then immediately reassures Abram, saying:

> This shall not be thine heir; but he that shall come forth out of thine own bowels shall be thine heir.
>
> And he brought him forth abroad, and said, Look now toward heaven, and tell the stars, if thou be able to number them: and he said unto him, So shall thy seed be.
>
> And he believed in the Lord; and he counted it to him for righteousness (Genesis 15:4-6).

WHAT DID ABRAM BELIEVE

Now what did God ask Abram to believe? He asked him to believe what He had said concerning a promised son. But more than that, God asked him to believe in a long-promised son, a long-delayed son, a miraculously born, a supernaturally given son. God asked Abram to believe the humanly impossible, the naturally unreasonable and the miraculously supernatural. When God fulfilled this promise to Abram he was one hundred years old, and his wife, Sarah, was ninety. They had both long since passed the time of life that they, in the course of nature, could expect to become parents of a child. Abram's body was "dead," we are told, as far as procreation was concerned. Sarah had long since passed the time of life for childbearing, and was maternally dead. It would, therefore, take a miracle to give them a child. It would have to be supernatural.

SARAH AND ABRAHAM WERE DEAD

In Genesis 18:11 we read this:

> Now Abraham and Sarah were old and well stricken in age; and it ceased to be with Sarah after the manner of women.

Abraham and Sarah were old and well stricken in years. That means that they were decrepit, senile, tottering in their old age. Sarah had long since passed the age of childbearing, for we read in God's Word that "it ceased to be with Sarah after the manner of women." In Hebrews 11:11 we read:

> Through faith, also Sara herself received strength to conceive seed, and was delivered of a child when she was past age, because she judged him faithful who had promised.

What was true of Sarah was true of Abraham also. He too had passed the years of fertility, and was sexually impotent to produce a child in the natural course of nature. The verses we quoted include Abraham as being old and well-stricken in years; and referring again to our opening Scripture in Romans 4, we gain the following interesting information. Speaking of Abraham, Paul says in Romans 4:18-22:

> Who against hope believed in hope, that he might become the father of many nations, according to that which was spoken, So shall thy seed be.
>
> And being not weak in faith, he considered not his own body now dead, when he was about an hundred years old, neither yet the deadness of Sarah's womb:
>
> He staggered not at the promise of God through unbelief; but was strong in faith, giving glory to God;
>
> And being fully persuaded that, what he had promised, he was able also to perform.
>
> And therefore it was imputed to him for righteousness.

Here, then, is the divine record itself. Abraham's body was dead; Sarah's womb was dead. Unless a miracle happened, they could have no children. But God promised a son and Abraham believed God's promise, even though it meant a miracle; and this faith saved him. The birth of Isaac was as great a miracle as the virgin birth of the Lord Jesus Christ, of whom he was only a type. Abraham believed God's Word concerning this son, and it was imputed unto him for righteousness.

For Us Also

What was true of Abraham is true today. Salvation and justification still come by believing God's Word concerning His Son, His miraculously conceived, supernaturally born Son. That is what John says in I John 5:9, 10:

> If we receive the witness of men, the witness of God is greater: for this is the witness of God which he hath testified of his Son.
>
> He that believeth on the Son of God hath the witness in himself: he that believeth not God hath made him a liar; because he believeth not *the record that God gave of his son.*

The truth here is as clear as it can be stated: Salvation is believing what God says about His Son, Jesus Christ. God knows of no other way of redemption for lost humanity.

The question at this point is, Have you believed on the Son of God? If you have, then you are saved. If you have not, then you are still in your sin. What is needed is not reason, not feeling, not emotion, but faith. Moreover, Abraham received no visions, emotions, or fleshly sensations, nothing but the promise of God in His Word. And this is God's way of salvation, for Paul ends the chapter on Abraham's faith in his Epistle to the Romans with these important words:

> Now it was not written for his [that is, Abraham's] sake alone, that it was imputed to him;
>
> But for us also, to whom it shall be imputed, if we believe on him that raised up Jesus our Lord from the dead;
>
> Who was delivered for our offences, and was raised again for our justification. (4:23-25).

CHAPTER ELEVEN

The Reward of Faith

> Abraham believed God, and it was counted unto him for righteousness.
>
> He staggered not at the promise of God through unbelief; but was strong in faith, giving glory to God;
>
> And being fully persuaded that, what he [God] had promised, he was able also to perform.
>
> And therefore it was imputed to him for righteousness (Romans 4:3; 20-22).

Faith is believing the unbelievable. Faith is believing the impossible and the unreasonable. Faith is believing something on the basis of the word of another. Faith is confidence in another's word and promise, though the word and promise be entirely beyond our reason and understanding. To have full faith in the promise of another, we must be convinced of his dependability and truthfulness, and his ability to carry out and fulfill his word and promise.

SAVING FAITH

Saving faith is believing God's Word, believing that He is trustworthy to fulfill His promise and able to carry it out. Faith is not reasoning about or feeling that Word, but simply believing it because God says it. That is why so few people are willing to believe God. They look for evidences, feelings, emotions and sensations, instead of putting simple faith and trust in the promises of the Lord. Abraham believed God, and was confident God could and would do as He said — give Abraham and Sarah a son in their old age.

The Virgin Birth

How the Lord brought about this miraculous birth of Isaac is fully revealed in Genesis 18. The aged Abraham received a call from the Lord as he rested in his tent at the middle of the day. After Abraham had welcomed his heavenly visitors, the Lord reveals to him how He is going to keep His promise of a son. The Lord says (Genesis 18:10):

> Where is Sarah thy wife? And he said, Behold, in the tent. And he [the Lord] said, I will certainly return unto thee according to the time of life; and, lo, Sarah thy wife shall have a son.

In these words we have God's own answer to the question of how He would perform this promise. He will set back the clock of time. He will make Sarah young again, and restore youth to this old, decrepit woman. That is the meaning of the statement:

> I will certainly return unto thee according to the time of life.

That is to say: "I will restore to Sarah the time of child-bearing. I will renew her youth, turn the clock back fifty or sixty years, and she will become a beautiful, virile, healthy, young woman again. I will restore her fertility, and the possibility of motherhood." He would do the same for Abraham and change this old, impotent man to virile, young manhood. That is God's word of explanation.

Sarah Laughs

Now Sarah hears these words of the Lord, and they strike her as very funny and utterly impossible. We read:

> Therefore Sarah laughed within herself, saying, After I am waxed old shall I have pleasure, my lord being old also (Genesis 18:12)?

This was too much for Sarah to believe, and so the Lord comes with a rebuke, and repeats the promise again:

> And the Lord said unto Abraham, Wherefore did Sarah laugh, saying, Shall I of a surety bear a child, which am old? Is anything too hard for the Lord (Genesis 18:13-14)?

Now notice God's answer again:

> At the time appointed I will return unto thee, according to the time of life, and Sarah shall have a son. (Genesis 18:14).

For the second time the Lord says, "I will restore to Sarah the time of childbearing and the time of life, and she shall become a mother." And God kept His promise. He brought about a transformation in Sarah which was wonderful. He took this old, stoop-shouldered, hobbling, wrinkled, gray-haired Sarah and completely transformed her. The gray hair turned black again, the wrinkles were all smoothed out, her stooped shoulders straightened up, her step became springy and youthful, the sparkle of youth returned to her eyes, and the color returned to her cheeks. This old woman became a beautiful, buxom young matron again.

ABIMELECH AND SARAH

If any of you are inclined to doubt this, and accuse me of indulging in wild imaginations, please reserve your criticism until we tell you the rest of the story. Some time after this, Abraham and Sarah made a journey to the country of Gerar (Genesis 20). I recommend that you read this chapter carefully. The king of Gerar was a man named Abimelech. Now something passing strange happens. This mighty king Abimelech of Gerar takes one look at Sarah and is so struck with her exceeding beauty that he immediately takes her as his wife. Here is the record:

> And Abraham journeyed from thence toward the south country, and dwelled between Kadesh and Shur, and sojourned in Gerar.
>
> And Abraham said of Sarah his wife, She is my sister: and Abimelech king of Gerar sent, and took Sarah (Genesis 20:1-2).

Now what is wrong here anyway? Here is an old woman, ninety years of age, of whom we read in Genesis 18 that she is "old and well-stricken in years," and long past the time of life of childbearing. And here is a mighty king who falls in love with this tottering old lady. The king of Gerar, who could have had the choice of all the fairest damsels in all his king-dom, falls in love with a stranger, a woman of ninety years. There is but one answer — God has done just as He had prom-ised, He has renewed Sarah's youth, He has returned unto her the "time of life." She is a beautful young woman again, possibly 25, 30 or 35; and the mighty King beholds her youth-ful beauty and chooses her above all others in his kingdom. How God prevented a tragedy you can read for yourselves in Genesis 20.

God Keeps His Promise

God always keeps His Word and fulfills His promise in a most wonderful and remarkable way. What He did for Sarah He also did for Abraham. We remind you again that the Bible says, "Abraham was old and well-stricken in years" before God began to work on him. Hebrews tells us that he was as good as dead. Then the Lord sets the clock back for Abraham also, and makes him a young man again. Isaac is born and grows up to manhood. As near as we can reckon, some forty years pass by, during which Sarah dies. And then comes the amazing record of Abraham at the age of about 140 years:

> Then again Abraham took a wife, and her name was Keturah.
> And she bare him Zimran, and Jokshan, and Medan, and Midian, and Ishbak, and Shuah (Genesis 25:1, 2).

An amazing record, indeed. Abraham becomes the father of a host of children, six sons are mentioned alone, and how many daughters there were is not mentioned. Abraham, an old man, his body dead, is restored to youth according to God's promise; and forty years afterwards we have this evidence that when God begins a work, He finishes it. He fulfills His promise that Abraham would not only be the father of the one covenant nation Israel, through Isaac, but also the father of many nations. All of this happens because Abra-ham believed what God said concerning a long-awaited, supernaturally given, miraculously born child.

I suggest you read the rest of the record of Abraham which

tells of his growth in faith, until it reaches a climax in Genesis 22 where he offers his only son upon the altar on Mt. Moriah.

PRACTICAL APPLICATIONS

Before I close, however, I would make some applications. The first is to the sinner. God has not changed since Abraham's day and His way of salvation has not changed in the least. He is still the same. Abraham by his first birth was lost, but God called him, and he believed. He believed what God said about his miraculously born son. And you, my sinner friend, must be saved the same way or be forever lost. You must believe, simply believe, what God says about His virgin born Son, the Lord Jesus, of whom Isaac was only a shadow and a type; you must believe not only in His death and in His resurrection but also in His miraculous birth. Believe Him today. Receive His Son, Jesus Christ, by faith, and be saved.

To the believer: I trust these messages have strengthened your faith. Surely we can trust Him, surely He is faithful. When the trials and tests of life come, let us remember Abraham's experiences. Even though everything be dark and there seems to be no way out, and our prayers go unanswered, and the burdens become heavier, we can believe that God is dealing with us and permitting, yes, even sending, trials and tribulation in order to train, discipline and prepare us for even greater blessings and victories, and to make us more like the Lord Jesus, who Himself was not made perfect without sufferings.

God grant us faith and grace to trust Him always, in every trial of life, and ever be able to say:

> I will not doubt though all my ships at sea
>   Come sailing home with tattered mast and sail.
> I will believe the Hand which cannot fail,
>   From seeming evil worketh good for me.
> And though I weep because those sails are tattered,
>   Still I'll cry while my last hopes lie shattered,
>   I'll trust in Thee.

I will not doubt though all my prayers return
  Unanswered from the still white realm above.
I will believe it was an all-wise love
  That has refused these things for which I yearn.
And though at times I cannot keep from grieving
  Still the pure ardor of my fixed believing
          Undimmed shall burn.

I will not doubt though sorrows fall like rain
  And troubles swarm like bees around a hive.
I will believe the heights for which I strive
  Are only reached through anguish and through pain.
And though I writhe and groan beneath my crosses,
  I still shall reap through my severest losses
          The greater gain.

I will not doubt, well-anchored in this faith.
  Like some staunch ship my soul braves every gale.
So strong its courage that it will not quail
  To meet the mighty unknown sea of death.
Oh, may I cry while body parts with spirit,
  "I will not doubt, I will not doubt," so list'ning worlds
    may hear it,
          With my last breath.

*This is the victory that overcometh the world, even our
faith* (I John 5:4).

CHAPTER TWELVE

The Assurance of Faith

> Lord God, whereby shall I know that I shall inherit it (Genesis 15:8).

In the previous chapter we have seen that Abraham was saved solely and completely and exclusively by believing the Word of God concerning the supernaturally and miraculously born, long-promised son. Abram, therefore, was saved by faith and not by works. But soon after Abram had believed God, doubts began to arise in his mind, and he began to wonder as to the absolute certainty of that which he had accepted. He still lacked the full assurance. Abram was of like passions as we are, and like many of God's children today, he sought for something in addition to that which God had plainly spoken. If you are like that, I invite you to give careful attention to the story of Abram as it is continued in chapter 15 of Genesis.

Yes, Abram had believed, but soon doubts begin to arise in his mind, and he seems to say, "Lord, if I only had some more evidence, some external evidence that I could see; if I had not only your word, but something in addition to your own word, it would make me feel a great deal better." You see, Abram would like to have had some emotional evidence, or some manifestation or sign, possibly of the flesh, so that he could say, "Now I know that I am saved." There are many today also who want to see things happen or to have some sensation of the flesh or the mind, who are seeking for something in addition to the simple Word of

God. Now Abram may have been looking for some sort of evidence of that kind. He says, in verse 8:

> Lord God, whereby shall I *know* that I shall inherit it (Genesis 15:8)?

PICTURE OF CALVARY

God had taken him out into the night and shown him the stars of heaven, and promised him, "so shall thy seed be." There was the simple promise, unattended by any other evidence. God had said to Abram, "I am the Lord that brought you out of the Ur of the Chaldees to give you this land to inherit it." And Abram says, "I know, and I believe it the best I can, but I do desire something additional whereby I shall *know* that I shall inherit this land." Then follows one of the most profound and marvelous pictures in answer to Abram's cry for more assurance:

> And he said unto him, Take me an heifer of three years old, and a she goat of three years old, and a ram of three years old, and a turtledove, and a young pigeon.
>
> And he took unto him all these, and divided them in the midst, and laid each piece one against another: but the birds divided he not.
>
> And when the fowls came down upon the carcasses, Abram drove them away (Genesis 15:9-11).

God gives him this wonderful picture and continues in verse 17 and 18:

> And it came to pass, that when the sun went down, and it was dark, behold a smoking furnace, and a burning lamp that passed between those pieces.
>
> In the same day the Lord made a covenant with Abram, saying, Unto thy seed have I given this land, from the river of Egypt unto the great river, the river Euphrates.

Abram had asked God for the assurance of the promises of God. Probably, as we suggested before, he was looking for some unusual manifestation, some physical experience, or some other external evidence by which he would be able to say, "Now I can be certain that God has really spoken." But instead of this, God takes Abram to Calvary and seems to say, "The only sign I am going to give you is a picture of Calvary. If you can stand before Calvary and see all that I have done there, and then still have any doubts in your mind, there isn't anything else that I can do for you." He tells him to take a heifer three years old, a she goat three years old, a ram three years old, a turtledove and a pigeon; and He commands Abram to slay them.

Now it is worthy of note that the only part Abram had in this entire transaction described here was simply putting to death the sacrifice. It is important to see this. Every one of these animals and these birds is a type and a picture of the redemptive work of the Lord Jesus Christ. The heifer has to do especially with the cleansing of salvation; the ram with the atonement; the goat with the carrying away of our sins into the wilderness; and the pigeon and the turtledove with the keeping power of Almighty God in sanctification. It is a marvelous, wonderful picture of the Lord Jesus Christ who had to be slain by the hand of the sinner; but beyond that, like Abram, the sinner has absolutely nothing to do at all in the procuring of redemption.

Abram takes the heifer, and cuts it in two and lays one piece over on one side, and the other piece opposite. Then he takes the goat, cuts it in two and lays one half on one side, and the second piece opposite the first. Then he takes the ram and does the same with it, a half on one side and a half on the other. The birds he divides not, but places them in their entirety, one on each side, so that the result is an aisle or a passageway between these bloody pieces of the sacrifice, through which, as we shall see later on, and upon the basis of which, God is going to give Abram the answer to his question regarding the assurance and the knowledge of salvation.

Covenant Confirmation

Such a procedure was one of the methods in olden times of confirming a covenant. When the ancient orientals came together to make an agreement, they had different ways of doing it. For instance, we read in the Bible concerning a covenant of salt. They would sit down and eat salt together, and that was a pledge of covenant relationship. Sometimes confirmation took the form of the striking of the hand. We call it a "handshake." We make an agreement together and say, "All right, this thing is settled; here's my hand; let's shake on it." That is a confirmation of an agreement and of a covenant. But there was another, far more dramatic way of confirming a covenant. This method was followed when two parties made an agreement or covenant of great importance. They would take an animal, a clean animal, quite often a calf, cut it in two and lay the pieces opposite each other. Then the two parties to this covenant would meet between these bloody pieces, join hands, and standing between the bleeding carcass, would repeat something like this. "Let it be done unto him who breaketh this covenant as was done unto this animal. Let him die the death." That action then became the confirmation of the covenant.

Abram and God are following a similar procedure. Such an act of confirmation is also mentioned in Jeremiah 34:18-20. Here God is finding fault with those who have broken His agreement:

> And I will give the men that have transgressed my covenant, which have not performed the words of the covenant which they had made before me, when they cut the calf in twain, and passed between the parts thereof,
>
> The princes of Judah, and the princes of Jerusalem, the eunuchs, and the priests, and all the people of the land, which passed between the parts of the calf;
>
> I will even give them into the hand of their enemies, and into the hand of them that seek their life: and their dead bodies shall be for meat unto the fowls of the heaven, and to the beasts of the earth.

God here promises judgment upon the nation of Israel because it had broken His covenant made between the pieces of the sacrifice.

Picture of the Sinner

Coming back to Abram, we notice that after the sacrifice had been slain by Abram and the parts divided and laid one over against the other, Abram falls asleep:

> And when the sun was going down, a deep sleep fell upon Abram; and, lo, an horror of great darkness fell upon him (Genesis 15:12).

It is as though God said, "Now listen, Abram, you must get out of the way first. You have nothing to do whatsoever with the part that is to follow now. This is something that I am going to do all by Myself, and I would like to have you get out of the picture completely." So God gave Abram an anesthetic, put him to sleep and gave him a bad dream while he was asleep, for we read that "an horror of great darkness fell upon him."

We recognize immediately here the picture of the sinner before Almighty God. The Lord is now to demonstrate His wonderful salvation by His matchless grace, and He says, as it were, first of all, "You must be out of the picture entirely. You have not one single thing you can do or should do. You cannot lift a finger toward your own salvation. You are totally dead in trespasses and in sins, helpless and paralyzed and blind. Therefore you must be set aside first or you will spoil the entire transaction." There is nothing the sinner can do at all. Essentially, he cannot even believe until he has been quickened by the Holy Spirit to believe.

Salvation is the work of God, and so the Lord tells Abram to get out of the picture entirely. He sets aside the sinner and puts him under the darkness of condemnation and under the awful blackness of the horror of the wrath of Almighty God.

The Furnace and the Lamp

After God has removed Abraham completely out of the picture, this is the record we read:

> And it came to pass, that, when the sun went down, and it

was dark, behold a smoking furnace, and a burning lamp that passed between those pieces (Genesis 15:17).

This transaction, we are to remember, is in Abram's behalf, but we are also to remember that Abram himself had nothing to do with it. This is being done entirely by another and that one is represented as a smoking furnace and a burning lamp, passing together between the pieces of a slain sacrifice.

Among the many attributes of God, we have two main classifications of attributes which we may best designate as the "justice of God" and the "love of God." The first group of attributes, including His justice, truth, righteousness, all demand the death of the sinner. But the second group of attributes, His love and mercy, long-suffering and compassion, demand the salvation of those whom He has chosen. How to satisfy both of these infinite demands is the problem of Calvary. The smoking furnace speaks of God's eternal wrath. Every time we read in the Bible about smoke, it means judgment. When Sodom and Gomorrah were destroyed, Abram saw the smoke of judgment ascending from the city. When God came down in judgment upon Sinai to give the law, the whole mountain was in smoke. When John sees the lost condemned in the pit of hell, he says, "The smoke of their torment ascendeth up forever and ever." Contrasted to the smoke, we have here the light, a burning lamp which dispels the darkness of judgment.

We have, then, the smoking furnace of God's wrath, and the burning lamp of God's love. We have God's justice demanding the death of the transgressor, and the infinite love of God seeking the redemption of that poor sinner. How these two can be satisfied is the problem of Calvary. The angels, of course can not solve it. How then will it be done? Someone has very aptly called this "the problem of the atonement." God's wrath demands that the sinner shall die, according to His Word, and pay the penalty of eternal death and separation. But if God satisfies His justice, His love is violated, and love seems to come and say, "No, I demand that he shall be with me forever and that he shall be saved." So we have this problem, justice saying, "No," and love saying, "Yes."

We cannot solve it, because we have no analogy in our own life that can begin to compare with this act of God on Calvary. I may say to my child, "Now if you do this or do that, I am going to spank you. I'm going to use the razor strap on you." But when he comes in after having disobeyed me, he knows how to handle dad. He manufactures a couple of tears, his lip begins to tremble, and instead of getting the rod, I pick him up in my arms and hug and kiss him, and forgive him. By doing so, however, I have made myself a liar. I have violated my promise. I have said that I would punish him, and I did not do it. I have broken my promise of punishment.

Now, beloved, God cannot do anything of that kind because He is unchangeable. He Himself has said, "In the day thou eatest thereof thou shalt surely die." He also said, "The wages of sin is death." He *must* punish the sinner with an infinite punishment, which means that it would take man an eternity to pay the price.

There is, however, also love, just as powerful, just as infinite, because all of God's attributes are equal. It says, "No, if justice acts, then love will be violated." Now how is this problem going to be met? The sinner cannot meet it, and so God comes and says, as it were, "I will pay man's debt myself in the person of a sacrifice, even my Son, the Lord Jesus Christ," who alone is able to meet this problem.

Think now of God passing between the sacrifice while Abram is asleep and helpless. There you have a picture of Calvary. Because He was infinite God, He could pay the infinite penalty for man. Thus we have the smoking furnace, God satisfied, in the sacrifice of these bleeding animals, while Gods love also is fully satisfied on the basis of this same sacrifice. "Mercy and truth are met together, righteousness and

peace have kissed each other" at Calvary. God's justice fully
satisfied in the death of His Son, God's wrath met, and at the
same time His love fully gratified on the basis of the sacrifice
of an innocent substitute. Abram himself should have lain
there on the altar; that was his proper place. Instead God permitted him to kill an innocent substitute. Then He stood between the pieces of the sacrifice and made His covenant of
pure grace; He joined hands as it were with Himself, for
the salvation of Abraham. When it is done, He seems to say,
"Now, Abram, wake up; I have good news for you." We are
not surprised that immediately after this incident we read:

>   In the same day the Lord made a covenant with Abram
>   (Genesis 15:18).

God's Word and God's Son

If we read on and discover the content of the covenant, we
have further evidence of the grace of God. We read:

>   Unto thy seed *have* I given this land.

This is the first time that God says, "Unto thy seed *have* I
given the land." Up until now it had been a promise; now it
becomes an established fact. God speaks as though it were already done. And so too the Christian today, who seeks for assurance, can but go to Calvary where God seems to say,
"There is the evidence of my love. If you can stand before
Calvary and still doubt that I love you, still doubt that My
Word is true, there is nothing else that I can possibly do for
you."

It must be impressed upon our minds that to ask for anything more than the simple word of the living God and Calvary is an insult to the Almighty and an example of our own
doubt. When Abram asked God for further assurance, God
gave him a picture of Calvary and confirmed His covenant.
Today there is a great tendency for men not to be satisfied
with the Word of God, but to look for other evidences,
emotional experiences and disturbances, mental experiences and
fleshly manifestations. Men want to have feelings and see

signs and wonders and miracles, and have all sorts of strange
dreams and visions and manifestations; but God says in effect,
"All these things are dishonoring to Me." He wants nothing
more than for us to believe the record of His Word. Again we
refer you to that passage in I John 5:9:

> If we receive the witness of men, the witness of God is
> greater: for this is the witness of God which he hath testified of
> his Son.
>
> He that believeth on the Son of God hath the witness in
> himself: he that believeth not God hath made him a liar;
> because he believeth not the record that God gave of his Son.

Let us be satisfied only with His Word and with the record
of what He has done through Jesus Christ. Can we, my
friends, stand before Calvary and see the agony of the Son of
God as He hangs there upon the Cross, bleeding and dying in
our stead until out of the depth of the distress of His soul He
cries out, "Eli, Eli, lama sabachthani?," "My God, my God,
why hast thou forsaken me?" and realize that it was for us
that God gave His Son, that He should die and then still
doubt? Certainly we must see the awful sin of asking for
anything more than that which He has so clearly demonstrated on the Cross of Calvary. And so in answer to Abram's
question, "Whereby shall I know?", God said, "Go to Calvary." May the Lord bring us to Calvary day by day so that
we shall ask for nothing more than His Word.

CHAPTER THIRTEEN

The Seed of Abraham

> And I will establish my covenant between me and thee and
> thy seed after thee in their generations for an everlasting cove-
> nant, to be a God unto thee, and to thy seed after thee.
> And I will give unto thee, and to thy seed after thee, the
> land wherein thou art a stranger, all the land of Canaan, for
> an everlasting possession; and I will be their God (Genesis
> 17:7, 8).

In these two verses we have a restatement of the covenant
which God made with Abram concerning His seed and the
land which was to be the possession of his seed forever. I feel
like saying at the outset of this chapter, "What God hath
joined together let no man put asunder." Verse 7 and 8 belong together. It is customary for those who spiritualize the
Scriptures to quote Genesis 17:7 as a foundation for applying
Abram's covenant only to us in this day, and to build upon
this the false assumption that God is all through with the
literal seed of Abraham. However, if we remember that verse
8 follows verse 7, we find that God is speaking here definitely
concerning a physical seed and a physical land which was to
be that seed's possession forever and ever. I emphasize the
necessity of keeping the two verses together if we are to understand what God has in His wonderful purpose for the future.

A SEED AND A LAND

Notice, therefore, that the covenant which God made with
Abram centers around two things, a seed and a land. Over
and over again God mentions the land in Palestine. First He

speaks of "the land that I will show thee." Then in chapter 15 God mentions " a land which I have given to thee." In each instance where God speaks of the land, He associates with it the seed of Abram through Isaac. The seed and the land are inseparable. As long as the seed and the land are together, blessing must result, but as soon as the seed and the land are separated. chaos results. There can, therefore, never be peace on earth until the literal seed of Abraham is once again fully settled in the literal land of Canaan.

God had called Abram to be the father of a peculiar nation, after the nations of the world had failed. Through him all the rest of God's program must be carried on. The entire Bible, with the exception of very few books, was written by descendants of this man, Abram. The whole Old Testament from chapter 12 of Genesis on deals with him and with his seed. The New Testament has to do almost exclusively with Abraham's literal seed, and then with a spiritual seed which we shall see was included in the covenant promise which God made with Abram. The Bible, then, records first of all the history of the seed of Abram, not only his physical seed, the sands of the sea shore, but his heavenly seed, the stars of the heaven, and then a seed which should be as the dust of the earth.

When we turn to the record elsewhere in the Scriptures, we find that Abraham has three seeds, not only one, but three. The contradiction is resolved when we remember that the blessing of the three seeds centers around the one Seed, the Lord Jesus Christ, who gathers them all together. Every blessing which Israel has ever had is because of Him; every blessing the Church has ever enjoyed is because of Him; every blessing the world has ever enjoyed, and will ever enjoy, is because of Him. Christ then becomes the center of it all as the seed of Abraham, and every blessing of God is because of Him. Even those who do not acknowledge Him, even those who curse Him, even those who have no use for Him are still here breathing air and drinking water and eating food and enjoying God's sunshine and life because of the greater Seed of Abraham, the Lord Jesus Christ Himself.

THREE KINDS OF PEOPLE

Here indeed is a tremendous truth. I would like to have you notice, that since the blessing of this seed is to be upon all nations and all the world, this seed must include all people. Now there are only three kinds of people in the world today. We have many classifications of people according to color, social standing, nationality, religion and so forth. The Bible, however, recognizes only three kinds of people living in the world today. Paul tells us in I Corinthians 10:32:

> Give none offence, neither to the Jews, nor to the Gentiles, nor to the church of God.

This text includes the only three kinds of people who are in the world, dispensationally. Redemptively, there are only two kinds of people — saved and lost; but dispensationally, there are three — the Jew, the Gentile and the church of God. Now the Jew is the natural, physical descendant of Abraham through Isaac, Jacob and the twelve tribes of Israel, collectively he is usually known as Israel. A Gentile is anyone else, no matter what color or race he may be; who is not a Jew and not a descendant of the twelve tribes of Israel. A member of the church of God is either a Jew or a Gentile, for it makes no difference, who by faith in the finished work of the Lord Jesus Christ becomes a member of the one true Church which is His Body.

I think it is an evil, bigoted, hypocritical and Pharasaical doctrine which would make any one certain, bigoted denomination the Body of Christ alone, and the rest of us who do not belong to it either shut out or merely "friends of the Bridegroom." What a stench this bigotry must be in the nostrils of Almighty God. A Christian, a believer in the Lord Jesus, is a member of the Body of Christ and of the Bride of Christ.

We have, then, three kinds of people in the world — the

might be better to say: "The light of the world
Today you and I are to be the light of the world,
s light in a dark and sin-sick age that is groping
no place to go. Unless you and I tell this world
it will never know about Him; for He is not the
world in the sense mentioned, except as we allow
e through our lives.

GREAT RESPONSIBILITY

Lord is depending upon us to shed light in this
darkness. If you and I do not show forth this
o not shed forth the glory of His face, the world
now about Him. How important, therefore, that
ght shine before men. We may talk about revival,
on meetings, we can shout and yell and tear our
until the world sees something more than what
hear us say, they are not going to believe us.
king for some evidence of light, they are groping
You and I are the only ones who have the lamp
How little we have done so far. We have been
other things, with material things, with business,
money, with pleasure, with everything else, that
s not been able to see the difference between us
and themselves as unbelievers.

y God have mercy upon us. There are some of
e not prayed for a soul for days and for weeks.
t won a soul for Christ since — you do not remem-
ou have not been burdened as you ought to be.
ess this upon your hearts. The world is sick of
preach. They want to see some more light and
d really consistent, Godly living.

lition to a "sand" seed and a "starry" seed, Abra-
o to be the father of a seed compared to the *dust*
This refers clearly to the nations of the world
rred to repeatedly as "dust." (Isaiah 26:19 and
) After Jesus comes to take His Church, the

Jew, the Gentile and the church of God. This was also true
in the days before the flood. In chapter 24 of Matthew, Jesus
says, "As in the days that were before the flood . . . so
shall also the coming of the Son of man be." Our Lord not
only said, "As it was in the days of Noah" but also as in the
days that were *before* the flood . . . "so shall also the coming
of the Son of man be." Among many other things, then, we
find this great truth that there were just three kinds of people
at that time also. This truth, of course, makes a wonderful
prophetic picture of the coming of the Lord.

First of all there was one who was raptured before the
flood. Then there were some who went through the flood and
came out safely upon a renewed earth, and then there was a
third great company who perished in the flood. Remember
that: One was taken out before, some went through, and
others perished in the flood. Enoch, type of the church of the
Lord Jesus Christ, was taken out before the flood, which, of
course, we know is a shadow of the tribulation period. Noah
and his family represent God's nation, Israel, faithfully brought
through the flood and planted upon a renewed, refreshed, re-
juvenated earth. And then the great mass of those who had
heard the message, and who all perished in the flood represent
the nations of today who have turned their backs upon the
Lord Jesus. "So shall also," said our Lord, "the coming of
the Son of man be."

THREE KINDS OF SEED

Now all of that is true today according to the words of our
Saviour and we have again these same three groups, and these
three groups correspond to the three seeds included in the
blessing of Abraham. We have three figures of the seed given
by God to Abraham. First of all, Abraham's seed is compared
to the sands of the sea shore (Genesis 22:17). Then we have,
secondly, God saying to Abraham, "Look now toward heaven,
and tell the stars, if thou be able to number them . . . So shall
thy seed be" (Genesis 15:5). This we call the "starry seed"

or the "glory seed." Then there is a third reference where God says that the seed of Abraham should be as the *dust* of the earth (Genesis 13:16). The blessing of Christ has a definite application and relation to every one of these three seeds — sand, stars and dust.

Someone has pointed out that the *sand* seed is Israel. Sand upon the sea shore is nothing else but pulverized and crushed rock. Throughout the ages the shifting tides from the ocean currents have jostled the rocks against each other. Large and small pieces were chipped off. Then the waves and the surf beat them back and forth, back and forth, until throughout the countless ages, these rocks have been reduced to fine sand on the shore of the sea. What a prophetic picture of Israel, scattered these twenty-five hundred years among the Gentile nations, driven from pillar to post, beaten, crushed, maligned, persecuted, forsaken by everything and everyone but God apparently, and ground finer and finer in their national pride. When God is all through with them, He is once more going to cast them out upon the shores of Palestine, as the sea shore seed. Now that, of course, is the first application here when God says, "In Isaac shall thy seed be called." Israel today, ground fine into humility, is beginning to emerge from the sea of the nations and I believe, soon will be restored, not only nationally, but spiritually, into the land of their promise.

Then there comes the second blessing. God says that not only through this seed of Abraham which is Christ will there be a sand seed, but there will be a *starry* seed, like the stars of the heaven. I am often greatly blessed by contemplating the beautiful figure of stars. As Daniel tells us, "They that turn many to righteousness shall shine as the stars forever." I do not know of a more beautiful picture of the members of the Body of Christ.

No Other Light

It is true of the church, the members of the Body of Christ, that they are already seated in the heavenlies. It is true that

---

they are dead with Him, buried, raised, ascended, and of God in the heavenlies. earth. There are too many with their position in heaven earth as they ought. There business of Christians, first the heavenlies, is to shine he has no other light than the liever in the Lord Jesus Chri

> The whole world was
> The light of the worl

But that is not strictly true. is based, we have a greatly study carefully chapter 9 of of the blind man, you will fi statement in verse 5:

> As long as I am in world.

Notice those words: "As long light of the world." Only a away, and He has not come He spoke here, Jesus Christ is Let me repeat, Jesus said; " am the light of the world." A "When I leave this world, I of the world, in the same se went away, He called His d them: "Ye are the light of t Myself am going away, but The world will not be able they see me now. I will not my light to be shed by you, Me." That is a truth for C quite the entire truth when

is Jesus." It *was* Jesus." reflecting Hi about with about Him, light of the Him to shin

Today the old world of light, and d will never k we let our li we may put hair out; bu they merely They are lo in darkness. of salvation. so busy with with making the world ha as believers

Truly, ma you who ha You have no ber when. May I impr hearing men testimony an

But in ad ham was als of the earth who are ref Isaiah 40:15

star seed, to glory, and restores His *sand* seed, Israel, to the land, then shall come the blessing of Abraham upon the *dust* seed, when the nations shall be blessed through the seed of Abraham, when

> Christ shall have dominion,
> Over land and sea;
> Earth's remotest regions,
> Shall His empire be.

Then shall be fulfilled the words of Isaiah 2:3 and 4

> And many people shall go and say, Come ye, and let us go up to the mountain of the Lord, to the house of the God of Jacob; and he will teach us of his ways, and we will walk in his paths: for out of Zion shall go forth the law, and the word of the Lord from Jerusalem.
>
> And he shall judge among the nations, and shall rebuke many people: and they shall beat their swords into plowshares, and their spears into pruninghooks: nation shall not lift up sword against nation, neither shall they learn war any more.

And again, Micah 4:3 and 4

> And he shall judge among many people, and rebuke strong nations afar off; and they shall beat their swords into plowshares, and their spears into pruning hooks: nation shall not lift up a sword against nation, neither shall they learn war any more.
>
> But they shall sit every man under his vine and under his fig tree; and none shall make them afraid: for the mouth of the Lord of hosts hath spoken it.

In that glorious day sickness will be unknown, poverty forever banished, and the nations of the world shall enjoy the long-hoped-for, and long-dreamed-of age of prosperity and blessing under the reign of King Jesus. May God hasten that glad day in answer to our prayer, "Even so, Come, Lord Jesus."

CHAPTER FOURTEEN

The Covenant of Grace

> In the same day the Lord made a covenant with Abram, saying, Unto thy seed have I given this land, from the river of Egypt unto the great river, the river Euphrates (Genesis 15:18).

God, in these words repeats His covenant of grace made with Abram after Abram had had a vision of Calvary in answer to his question, "Whereby may I *know* that I shall inherit it [the land]?" It is well that we remember the background and the occasion of the answer of God to Abram's request for more assurance. You will recall that God told him to prepare the slain animals; and while he was fast asleep, God passed between them in the form of a smoking furnace and a burning lamp, thus completing a beautiful picture of reconciliation at Calvary. After this picture of Calvary, God renews the covenant in the words which I have quoted.

ONLY TWO COVENANTS

In this chapter we digress in the story of Abram to say a little about the two covenants in the Word of God. Basically, there are only two covenants in the Bible. There can be no other than a covenant of works and a covenant of grace. All the other covenants mentioned in Scripture — the Edenic or Adamic, the Noahic, the Palestinian, or whatever we may have — are either of grace or works. A covenant of works is an agreement between God and man which depends for its blessing not only upon God's faithfulness, but also upon man's faithfulness and obedience. Every covenant of works always fails because it depends upon man. Anything which depends upon man must fail. All of the covenants of works in the Bible fail because they depend upon man.

Take, for instance, the covenant which God made with Adam in the garden of Eden, when God said, "Of every tree in the garden thou mayest freely eat, but of the tree of the knowledge of good and evil, thou shalt not eat of it: for in the day that thou eatest thereof thou shalt surely die," (Genesis 2:16, 17). That was a covenant of works, and depended for its success on Adam's obedience. We know the story of how Adam broke it. Or we may take the Palestinian covenant, given in such detail in both Leviticus and Deuteronomy. God in effect says to Israel, as a nation, "If you will behave yourself and keep my statutes and my laws, then I will bless you. But if you disobey, I will scatter you and judge you." The history of Israel throughout all the centuries is the evidence of their failure to abide by that covenant of works.

ONE EFFECTIVE COVENANT

A covenant of grace, however, never fails, because a covenant of grace is made by and with God Himself. In chapter 3 of Genesis God declares that He would put enmity between the woman and the serpent, between her seed and the seed of the serpent. Now we all know that God has kept His covenant, for it depended upon God's faithfulness alone. Man had nothing to do with the carrying out of it. After the flood, God came again to Noah, and said to Noah, "While the earth remaineth, seed time and harvest, and cold and heat, and summer and winter, and day and night shall not cease" (Genesis 8:22). God did not say, "If you behave yourself and follow in my footsteps, it will be so." He did not say, "It will continue upon condition of your obedience." Ah, no. This is a covenant of grace: it is what God is going to do in spite of anything anyone else may do; and that covenant which God made with creation has never been broken.

We are to recognize this, that a covenant of grace cannot
and will never be broken because all of it depends upon the
faithfulness of God. If we are under the covenant of works,
and under the law, we necessarily must be lost, because man
cannot keep it. If our salvation depends either upon our faithfulness or upon our behaviour, we are still lost; for it must be
grace and all of grace, from beginning to end. It must be the
work of God and God alone. The life of Abraham illustrates
this in a most dramatic way. Abraham had to learn that
lesson. God put him out of the way when the smoking furnace and the burning lamp passed between the pieces of the
sacrifice. We ought to thank God for the covenant of grace,
that it is one which is engineered entirely by the Almighty. It
is an agreement which God makes with Himself among the
three persons of the Trinity, Father, Son, and Holy Spirit,
whereby He promises and determines to do something for
someone else, wholly and entirely independent of any action
or conduct on the part of the one for whom He performs it.

Every believer, every individual is either under grace or
he is under the works of the law. If under the works of the
law, then the Bible says, "Cursed is everyone that continueth
not in all things written in the book of the law to do them"
(Galatians 3:10). That is God's Word. It does not tell us
to do our best, but it demands absolute obedience and perfection. Nothing less than perfection can ever avail. If the
individual is under grace, he is to remember that a covenant
of grace depends basically upon God's faithfulness, not upon
his faithfulness. It is not the strength of his faith, be it ever
so mighty, but it is the strength of God's Word and promise
which keeps him. I re-emphasize that it must be the faithfulness of God.

The Security of Believers

A covenant of grace means, then, that God promises and
does something independently of anything that the object of
that grace may do. God says, "I will." In the first statement

of the covenant which God made with Abraham back in Genesis 12, He repeats the expression, "I will," no less than seven times. In the passage which we have in chapter 15, God has changed the tense, and says to Abram: "Unto thy seed *have* I given this land." In other words, God says, on the basis of Calvary, that it is all settled, it is all done. It is already accomplished. You are as good as in heaven, and if you have trusted the Lord Jesus Christ as your personal Saviour, on the basis of His substitutionary death and resurrection, you today are as secure as you will be ten billion years after Jesus comes. That certainly is the force of the words of this covenant: "Unto thy seed *have* I given this land."

Now if we turn for a moment to Hebrews, we find in the sixth chapter, verses 13 and 14, another statement which bears upon this same truth in a remarkable way:

> For when God made promise to Abraham, because he could swear by no greater, he sware by himself,
>
> Saying, Surely blessing I will bless thee, and multiplying I will multiply thee.

This agreement, this covenant, then, was made with God Himself. It was made in behalf of Abraham but He would not dare let Abraham have anything to do with it. It would not work if He had, so He sware by Himself,

> Saying, Surely blessing I will bless thee, and multiplying I will multiply thee.
>
> And so, after he had patiently endured, he obtained the promise.
>
> For men verily swear by the greater: and an oath for confirmation is to them an end of all strife.
>
> Wherein God, willing more abundantly to shew unto the heirs of promise the immutability of his counsel, confirmed it by an oath:
>
> That by two immutable things, in which it was impossible for God to lie, we might have a strong consolation, who have fled for refuge to lay hold upon the hope set before us (Hebrews 6:14-18).

We have here two immutable things. God must satisfy His immutable justice in the death of the sinner before His love can be satisfied in the salvation of the sinner. These are the two immutable things mentioned in Genesis 15, the smoking furnace and the burning lamp; the unchangeable justice and the unchangeable love of God. In our age, when theology is so often superficial and shallow, we hear but little about these basic things of salvation. We talk a great deal about the love of God, but the background of Calvary is judgment; and the blacker we paint the background of God's wrath, the brighter the love of God will of necessity stand out in bold relief. Until there is a sense of condemnation and conviction of sin, we shall never be able to have revival. We are never going to get it by mushy, watered-down, compromising popular dissertations on the love of God. Revival can never come that way. It will come only when some of us will dare to get up and preach hell and damnation and the wrath of God and eternal punishment once again. We can go into the history of any revival, and we will find that the preachers preached the wrath of God with all their heart, and then preached the love of God against this background. God's love, unless it is presented against the background of God's righteousness and holiness, becomes a weak and powerless message. His love, the burning lamp, is not sufficient; we must also have the smoking furnace, by which it was impossible for God to save the sinner in any way without satisfying His righteousness as well.

This, then, was God's answer to Abram's question, "How shall I *know?*", his question for full assurance. God seems to say, "Go to Calvary, go to Calvary. Stand before Calvary and see what I have done. If you can stand before Calvary and see what I have done there, how I exhausted heaven of its wisdom in order to bring about this marvelous plan of salvation, for it did take infinite wisdom, and infinite love and infinite mercy, if you can stand there and then still doubt that I love you, there is nothing more that I can do."

AT CALVARY

When we were lost and in sin and wallowing in the mire, God in great and wonderful compassion and love devised this scheme and sent His precious Son, the Lord Jesus, all the way from glory. He came here, the infinite God, Creator of the universe, who made the worlds by simply speaking a word, the stars and constellations and all the systems and galaxies more easily than I can snap my finger. That great Creator laid aside the form of God and stepped down to the lowest depths to save us. While the angels stood in admiration and adoration and awe, He came down, down, down past all the greater stars and blazing planets until He stopped upon an infinitesimally small clod of dirt we call the earth. Here this great, eternal God took up His abode in a microscopic human cell, planted Himself in the womb of a virgin Jewish mother, and dwelt under the pulsating heart of a human mother for nine whole months, gathering his nourishment from humanity whom He came to save. At the end of that He was born through blood and tears and pain a weeping babe, and had to be nursed at a human breast. He had to learn to walk and talk, and yet veiled within Him for the purpose of redeeming the very ones who were to put Him to death was infinite God.

Then He went and worked with His hands and became like unto us in all things, sin excepted. For a brief period of three and one-half years, He is despised, rejected, laughed at, scorned, mocked, reviled, connived against, schemed against, until at last they take Him to Calvary, the Son of God, and stretch Him out upon the Cross, nail His hands and His feet to a tree and raise Him up between two thieves as they cry out, "If you are the son of God, come down from the Cross." The awful piercing thorns cut into His blessed scalp as He hangs there with every muscle tense, His lips pinched with the pain and the agony; while the great sorrow that is breaking His heart is that of the sin which God has laid upon Him, not His own sin, but ours. His eyes stare in consternation at the awful prospect of God Himself plunging Him into the darkness where sinners ought to be, until at last, His body covered like a robe of crimson with His own precious blood, writhing on the Cross, God Himself is unable to behold the awful spectacle, and closes His almighty eyes, shuts His ears to the cry of His own beloved Son, as He rends the air with, "My God, My God, why hast Thou forsaken Me?" And He did it all that we might be saved.

Do Not Ask For More

I want to ask you, in the name of our Saviour: Can you stand before Calvary, beloved, and ask for more evidence of His love for man? And I want to say again, kindly and tenderly in a spirit of helpfulness, that this miserable Satanic error which is gripping Christendom today by which men will not trust God until they see signs and wonders and look for something more than the record of God, is not of God, but of the devil himself. God is not a liar. God says in His Book, "Him that cometh unto Me, I will in no wise cast out."

> I came to Jesus as I was,
> Weary, worn, and sad;
> I found in Him a resting place,
> And He has made me glad.

Nothing can make us happier than trusting the Word of God. Yet such is the deception of the enemy that we are told that it is not enough only to believe God. We have to have further evidence. They say to us, "If you don't have what we have, how do you know that you are saved?" I know I am saved because God says it. "What saith the Scripture" is the answer. Abraham believed God.

So I come to you, precious friend, and ask you to believe Him. Only believe Him, and He will shower you with thrills and experiences and answers to prayer and things that are worth more than any signs or miracles. If you trust God wholly, completely, it is still to be seen what God will do for you. It is marvelous, but true: you do not need those things in order that you may trust Him first, but you get them because you do. "How shall I know?" said Abram to God, and God said, "Go to Calvary." When you are willing to do that, God comes in revelation. With that thought I would like to close this chapter. Going back to verses 13 through 16 of Genesis 15, I read:

> And he said unto Abram, Know of a surety that thy seed shall be a stranger in a land that is not theirs, and shall serve them; and they shall afflict them four hundred years;
>
> And also that nation whom they shall serve, will I judge: and afterward shall they come out with great substance.
>
> And thou shalt go to thy fathers in peace; thou shalt be buried in a good old age.
>
> But in the fourth generation they shall come hither again: for the iniquity of the Amorites is not yet full.

If we link up these verses with verse 18, "In the same day God made a covenant with Abram," then the very sin of unbelief and doubt will be gone forever. How it must grieve the Father's heart, how it must hurt Him, after all that He has done, that we should still doubt Him and ask for additional evidence, whatever it may be. I call upon you to trust Him. There is nothing that pleases the Father's heart more than to have His children put implicit trust in Him.

> Only trust Him, only trust Him,
> Only trust Him now.
> He will save you, He will save you,
> He will save you now.

CHAPTER FIFTEEN

The Lapse of Faith

> And Sarai Abram's wife took Hagar her maid the Egyptian, after Abram had dwelt ten years in the land of Canaan, and gave her to her husband Abram to be his wife.
>
> And he went in unto Hagar, and she conceived: and when she saw that she had conceived, her mistress was despised in her eyes.
>
> And Sarai said unto Abram, My wrong be upon thee: I have given my maid into thy bosom; and when she saw that she had conceived, I was despised in her eyes: the Lord judge between me and thee.
>
> But Abram said unto Sarai, Behold, thy maid is in thy hand; do to her as it pleaseth thee. And when Sarai dealt hardly with her, she fled from her face (Genesis 16:3-6).

This is the sad record of a man, a believer, a saint of God, who in a moment of weakness and doubt and impatience, succumbed to the temptation of the flesh. It was a terrible sin, the result of which plagued Abram to his dying day, and plagues his descendants to this very hour.

This sin of Abram proves that even in the Godliest saint there still lies the possibility of failure and sinning. The flesh is always there to overcome the child of God in a moment of carelessness. In a previous chapter I pointed out several examples of this. We saw that Jacob became Israel, but he never got rid of Jacob until he died. Simon became Peter, but Simon was never eradicated in this life. In the believer the Holy Spirit dwells, but the flesh is also still present. This is one of the most important truths for us to recognize if we are to gain Scriptural victory in our lives. There are too many people who have the idea that when they are saved, their troubles are all over. Beloved, that is when troubles start. Before we are saved, we have only the old nature, and there is no struggle. Very few people are mean enough to fight with themselves. But when we are saved, something, yea, Someone, moves in who is absolutely opposed to the old nature, and that is exactly when the fight begins. Undoubtedly that is what Paul meant when he said:

> For the flesh lusteth against the Spirit, and the Spirit against the flesh: and these are contrary the one to the other: so that ye cannot do the things that ye would (Galatians 5:17).

That is also why Paul said in Romans 7:19-21:

> For the good that I would I do not: but the evil which I would not, that I do.
>
> Now if I do that I would not, it is no more I that do it, but sin that dwelleth in me.
>
> I find then a law, that, when I would do good, evil is present with me.

And thirty-five years after Paul was saved, he was willing to admit:

> For I know that in me (that is, in my flesh,) dwelleth no good thing (Romans 7:18).

If there is anything we need to learn today, it is to recognize the enemy, not to ignore him, not to discount him, not to deny him; we need to recognize the presence within our own selves of the old nature along with the new nature.

Abram did not recognize this truth as he should, and had to learn it by a very bitter experience. All that God had to do to prove to Abram that he could not stand in his own strength was to delay the answer to His promise. The old man came to the surface immediately. Let the right circumstances come along, and you too will find it out, my friend, that within every saint there is still the potentiality of sinning. When people come to me and say, "My old nature is all gone and dead and eradicated," I simply ask, "Would

you like to have me talk to your wife about this matter?"
That usually ends the argument.

Flesh Is Flesh

Our Lord Jesus Himself said in speaking to Nicodemus:

> That which is born of the flesh is flesh; and that which is
> born of the Spirit is spirit (John 3:6).

That is a statement which ought to be studied carefully. Flesh
is flesh, and it can never be improved, and it can never be
changed. In the new birth, flesh does not become spirit, but
flesh remains flesh. It may be Presbyterian, or Baptist, or
Brethren or Congregational, or any kind of flesh. It may be
Italian, or Irish, or German, or American, but it is still sinful,
Adamic flesh. It may be black, or red, or pink, or yellow, or
any other kind of flesh, but it always will remain the flesh.
If we know our own hearts, we will say with Paul, "I know
that in me (that is, in my flesh,) dwelleth no good thing."

You are by your first birth so depraved, corrupt and hope-
less that even God will not seek to save the flesh. He seems
to say, "I'll have to make something brand new, and I'll put
that in, and it will give you the faith and the power to con-
quer the old." That is what God says. To work upon the
old man — that is what man himself tries to do. The Lord
allows man to try it by every conceivable means, but it always
ends in failure. Man tries to correct the old nature by
education, morality, understanding, teaching, conference, religion and things of that kind. Man speaks of his dignity,
the spark of divinity in him, which only needs a little develop-
ment, and of his inherent goodness; but God says:

> The heart is deceitful above all things, and desperately
> wicked: who can know it? (Jeremiah 17:9).

The old nature is so corrupt that God Himself will not
bother to do anything with it. The reason we have to be born
the second time, from above, is simply this, that the first
time we were born all wrong. It happens to be a physical
fact, and as a physician I can testify to this, having attended

hundreds and hundreds of childbirths, it happens to be an obstetrical fact that children normally come into the world upside down, physically upside down. Now, of course, we do not make too much of that fact, but it is suggestive at least of another fact — when God takes hold of a man, with his head already pointing downward toward hell, He turns him around and starts him upward toward heaven. God says:

> Except a man be born from above, he cannot see the kingdom of God (John 3:3).

KNOW THYSELF

Poor Abram gave way to the old nature of the flesh. I want to give a warning here to each and every one of us. The safest and the best thing that any believer can do is to recognize the presence of the flesh. I receive mail from people who tell me that they have not sinned for ten, fifteen or twenty years. All I can say to them is that this is absolutely contrary to the Word of God. It is contradicting the Almighty Himself. We are but to remember that sin is not an act, but sin is an attitude and a condition of the heart. Sin is not an action of the body or of the hand, but a condition of the human heart. Paul tells us, "All have sinned and come short of the glory of God," and Solomon tells us that "there is not a man that sinneth not." I do not know of a better definition of sin than the words of Paul, "coming short of the glory of God." Failing to attain, failing to measure up to God's perfect standard of Jesus Christ — that is sin. Anyone who has not yet attained the moral, spiritual and ethical perfection of Jesus Christ is still coming short of God's perfection; and that, says God, is sin. It may be merely the negative aspect of sin, but it is sin nevertheless. There is not anyone who will not still carry with him, until the day of his death, or the day of his glorification when Jesus comes, if he lives, all the potentialities of the old nature. And except by the grace of God these potentialities be kept down, the tragedy of Abram's life is too often repeated.

It happens to be a fact that a saint who has walked with God many, many years can sometimes fall to lower depths, and do meaner, more wicked things than the world would even think of doing. If you do not believe this, you have but to turn to the Word of God. Think of Peter as he cursed and denied his Lord. Think of Noah who became drunk after the flood, or Solomon, or David. The example of Abram in itself ought to prove it. He was the friend of God and the father of the faithful; yet he was willing to sell the honor of his own wife in order to save his own skin, in Egypt and again in Gerar. Even then he seems not to have learned his lesson. In chapter 16 we find him, at the age of 86, listening to the voice of Sarai as she tempts him, seeming to say: "God has forgotten all about his promise." He raises up a fleshly seed, Ishmael, which seed becomes a thorn in his own flesh, a sorrow in his tent and the occasion for malcontent, difficulty and misunderstanding in his own home. And today almost four thousand years later, the Arabs, the direct descendants of Ishmael, are still the traditional enemies of the Jews, the sons of Isaac. Abram lived in his tent for thirteen more long, barren years, because he could not wait, because his patience was exhausted, because he could not believe God to the end.

Now this is possible for every child of God today, and Paul therefore warns us:

> Wherefore let him that thinketh he standeth take heed lest he fall (I Corinthians 10:12).

I think that we ought to be extremely tender and gracious and longsuffering to those who do fall, realizing that we, except for the grace of God, would be in the same condition. Therefore I read this awful dark story in the life of Abram. We know that this story was recorded for our admonition. It is all a matter of which we allow to have the ascendency in our lives.

DECEIVING OURSELVES

You may say, "I don't believe this is the teaching of the Word of God," for I read in I John 3:9:

> Whosoever is born of God doth not commit sin; for his seed remaineth in him: and he cannot sin, because he is born of God.

People write in and ask, "What do you do with this? Does this not teach sinless perfection?" I certainly believe this to be the Word of God, but there happens to be another verse which John quotes before this one. We ought always to take things in their proper order. This previous verse occurs in chapter 1 of I John. There John is speaking about the very matter in question, and he says in verse 8.

> If we [not talking about sinners, but about himself and us] say that we have no sin, we deceive ourselves, and the truth is not in us.

John says that we are not fooling anyone; we are only deceiving ourselves. "We are deceiving ourselves, and the truth is not in us." This is a very serious accusation which John hurls at those who would claim that they are living without sin. It is as though God says, "You are not fooling me, for you have within you that which, no matter how by the grace of God it may be kept down by victory, is still able to sin." Furthermore, in verse 10 of this same chapter we read:

> If we say that we have not sinned, [again, *we*] we make him a liar, and his word is not in us.

The remedy is found in verse 9 which is placed right between the two verses already mentioned. We ought to face the truth as God has given it to us here:

> If we confess our sins, he is faithful and just to forgive us our sins, and to cleanse us from all unrighteousness.

OBJECTION OVERRULED

Someone may still object by quoting I John 3:9:

> Whosoever is born of God doth not commit sin; for his seed remaineth in him: and he cannot sin, because he is born of God.

I realize that many Bible teachers have tried to get out of the apparent difficulty by reading something into the verse which is not there. They tell us that it should read this way: "Whosoever is born of God does not 'practice' or 'continue in' sin." There are, however, two things wrong with this interpretation. First of all, it is not true to the text; and second, I would not dare to preach that a little sinning is not so bad, as long as we do not continue in it and practice it. That is to say, if we only play around with it a little, then we can dabble with sin, but we are not to go too far. I, for one, would never dare to preach a doctrine of that kind.

The word used in this verse for "commit sin" is *poeio*. The word for "practice" is *prasso*. Wherever the Bible means "practice," *prasso* is always used. The word *poeio* means to commit a single act of sin in distinction from *prasso* which means to practice sin continually. When John says, "Whosoever is born of God doth not commit sin," he uses the word *poeio*, not the word *prasso*. Then he goes on, "for his seed remaineth in him: and he cannot sin, because he is born of God." This man about whom John is talking not only never commits a single sin, but it is impossible for him to commit a single sin, because he is born of God. Now I hope that you will see what the answer is. In I John chapter 1, John is talking about the old Adam, the old man, which can do nothing else but sin. Concerning him John says, "If we say that we have no sin, we deceive ourselves, and the truth is not in us." But in I John 3:9 he is talking about the new nature of the believer, "that which is born of God," not that which is born of the flesh. This will become immediately apparent if you will look carefully at the verse. It begins and it ends with the same words: "Born of God." Evidently, then, John is talking about the new nature and the new man, that which is born of God, in distinction from the old nature and the old man, that which is born of the flesh. It is not necessary for us to twist the Greek words around to make them fit our theology, for fear that someone may have an argument. John recognizes the truth frankly, and says, "Whosoever is *born of God* doth not commit sin." Such a person is a partaker of the divine nature (I Peter 1:4).

Waiting Upon God

Abram had to find this out. We go back once more to Abram, before we conclude this chapter:

> Now Sarai Abram's wife bare him no children: and she had an handmaid, an Egyptian, whose name was Hagar.
>
> And Sarai said unto Abram, Behold now, the Lord hath restrained me from bearing: I pray thee go in unto my maid; it may be that I may obtain children by her. And Abram hearkened to the voice of Sarai (Genesis 16:1, 2).

Abram hearkened to the voice of the flesh. Through his impatience, thinking that God had delayed the answer to His promise too long, he took matters into his own hands. Ah, is not this the greatest temptation in the Christian life many times? The hardest test in our life is to wait for God's answer to our prayer and our desire. Impatience causes much sin, unbelief and grief. Yes, God answers prayer, but we can not order Him. He hears our petition, but we cannot tell Him how and when He is to answer our petitions. He reserves to Himself the privilege of determining the *when* and the *how*. Before Abraham could become the great example of overcoming, victorious faith that we find in chapter 22, when he sacrifices Isaac, he had to learn many lessons; and the greatest lesson he had to learn was that he in his own strength could do absolutely nothing.

Do you realize, Christian, that impatience is sin; that doubt is sin; that to be unwilling to take God at His Word and ask for more evidence is sin; that to take things into our own hands is sin. If you want victory in your life, there is only one way that it can be gotten. That way is to face frankly the truth that in your own strength you can do absolutely nothing, and then to say with Paul:

> I can do all things through Christ which strengtheneth me (Philippians 4:13).

CHAPTER SIXTEEN
Faith and Works

> Ye see then how that by works a man is justified, and not by faith only (James 2:24).

A series of messages on Abraham would be quite incomplete without some message on the matter of works in the life of the father of the faithful. For while we emphasize the fact that he was the great example of faith, works also entered very definitely into the life of this patriarch. Critics of the Bible, claiming there are many contradictions in the Scriptures, frequently assert that there is a conflict in the theology of Paul and the theology of James. They point to the fact that Paul claims that without exception a man is justified by faith alone, without the works of the law. However, James teaches very definitely that a man is justified by works as well as by faith. Since Paul and James both use the example of father Abraham to prove their particular points, it will be entirely proper, I am sure, to insert in this series on Abraham, a few chapters on the subject of "Faith and Works." I refer you again to Romans 4:1-4:

> What shall we say then that Abraham our father, as pertaining to the flesh, hath found?
>
> For if Abraham were justified by works, he hath whereof to glory; but not before God.
>
> For what saith the scripture? Abraham believed God, and it was counted unto him for righteousness.
>
> Now to him that worketh is the reward not reckoned of grace, but of debt.

There is no mistaking Paul's words in this passage. Works

have absolutely nothing to do with salvation, for it is all of faith. The harder we work, the deeper in debt we become. That is a terrible predicament to be in, but that is exactly what Paul says. Salvation is all of faith from beginning to the very end. If there is one thing which Paul insists upon, it is that works have nothing to do with the obtaining or the retaining of our salvation. We are justified by faith, and by faith alone. And so he adds a verse, Romans 4:5;

> But to him that worketh not, but believeth on him that justifieth the ungodly, his faith is counted for righteousness.

So insistent is Paul upon this fact that he states in the Epistle to the Galatians that the curse of Almighty God is upon all those who would add works to faith in the obtaining of salvation. In Galatians 1:8 we read:

> But though we, or an angel from heaven, preach any other gospel unto you than that which we have preached unto you, let him be accursed.

Paul is, of course, speaking concerning his Gospel, the Gospel of God's grace by faith without the works of the law, and he repeats this terrible condemnation in chapter 3 of Galatians, verse 10, where he says:

> Cursed is every one that continueth not in all things which are written in the book of the law to do them.

Justification, therefore, is by faith, wholly apart from the works of the law. But listen now to the Apostle James as he speaks in James 2:21 and 24, a passage which has caused a great deal of confusion among many believers in all ages. We read in these verses these amazing statements:

> Was not Abraham our father justified by works, when he had offered Isaac his son upon the altar?
>
> Ye see then how that by works a man is justified, and not by faith only.

APPARENT CONTRADICTION

There seems to be a contradiction. Paul has insisted that a man is justified by faith and faith alone, and James tells us just as emphatically that man is not justified by faith alone, but also by works; and both of them are equally emphatic in their statements. Even Martin Luther had difficulty with this verse in James. It is a well-known historical fact that after he had seen the truth of justification by faith, and that great verse, "The just shall live by faith," had blazed its light within his soul, He came in his study to the book of James. When he came upon this particular passage he simply could not reconcile the theology of Paul and the theology of James, and so for a time called James an epistle of straw and denied it a place in the authority and the canon of Scriptures.

We must first of all ask ourselves the question, What is God talking about and whom is He addressing? It is important that we do this if we are to divide the Word of truth rightly. All of the Bible was written *for* us, but not all of the Bible was written *to* us. While the entire Scripture has applications for us and a message for us, everything in Scripture certainly was not written for us to observe in its literal sense. The Lord told Israel to sacrifice animals, to observe various sabbath days and feast days, to circumcize their children, to destroy their enemies, to burn their cities and to do a thousand other things which certainly are not to be carried out literally by us today. Such orders do indeed contain lessons for us, but certainly are not primarily given to us to observe. What, then, is God talking about in Romans and in James? To whom is He speaking? If we will ask these questions concerning these two passages, I think we shall see a beautiful harmony which makes the balance of the Christian's life what God wants it to be.

Two Different Questions

Paul in Romans is discussing the question, How can a good-for-nothing, hell-deserving, hell-bound sinner be justified in the sight of a holy and a righteous God? The answer which Paul gives is this: "By faith and faith alone." Nothing else, nothing added, nothing taken away. Works have absolutely nothing to do with a man's justification in the sight of Almighty God.

James is talking about quite another matter. The question in James is this: "How can saints who are already justified in the sight of Almighty God, justify themselves in the sight of their fellow men?" And the answer to that question is: "Not by faith, but by works." In other words, God does not have to see our works to justify us, because He sees our hearts.

> For the Lord seeth not as man seeth; for man looketh on the outward appearance, but the Lord looketh on the heart (I Samuel 16:7).

The moment a poor, lost sinner cries in faith to God, from his heart, before his lips have spoken a word, before he has breathed a prayer, before he has done a single act to prove his faith, God has already reckoned that man saved, justified in His sight because He Himself is the Author of that faith. The moment that faith is within the heart, God sees that heart, and declares that man righteous and just in His sight. But now if nothing more than that happened, no one else except God would ever know about it. No one would ever suspect that this man was a believer. Before people can know that he has been justified in the sight of God, his faith must begin to operate in his life and become evident by his works, his conversation, his charity, his forgiveness, his longsuffering, his patience and all the other fruits of salvation. By these fruits, therefore, and works, he will give evidence of that which is already in his heart, and which God has already seen. Then only are men able to see that he is already justified in the sight of God, and consequently is now justified in the sight of men. God sees our faith, but man can only see our works, the evidence, the visible result of our faith.

We may sum it up like this, if you please. Faith is the root and our works are the fruit. The fruit of our faith is our works before men. James is talking about our justification

in the sight of men. Paul is talking about our justification in the sight of God.

Counting Converts

The Lord Jesus Christ said:

> Let your light so shine *before men*, that *they* may see your good works, and glorify your Father which is in heaven (Matthew 5:16).

God, I repeat, does not have to see our good works. He does not have to see any other evidence than faith in our heart. He does not have to see our light. There is nothing in the Word that indicates that God needs more than faith. Therefore Jesus says:

> Let your light so shine *before men*, that *they* may see your good works, and glorify your Father which is in heaven.

Only God knows, but we have to see. That is why — we say this graciously and kindly, and trust we will not be misunderstood — the popular practice of counting converts is contrary to the Word of God. We simply do not know who, or how many are saved. There are some who make a profession who have never trusted Christ. There are some who, because of conditions and circumstances, do not give as much evidence of their salvation as others do; God is the One who keeps the books. He is the One who does the counting. You and I have to wait until we see the works and the results before we can judge. I am definitely afraid that many of the people whom we have put down in our books as having been converted in our meetings will never show up in heaven, and we know from experience that there are countless others who have never been counted who are going to be in glory when the books are opened.

John and Joe

Permit me to illustrate this point. Suppose that we hold a meeting in your church, and at the close of the service when the invitation is given, two men come forward. For convenience we will call them Joe and John. From all appearances they are both under conviction. Of course, we know there are two kinds of conviction, a conviction of conscience, which is transient and never results in salvation, and a conviction of the Holy Spirit, which is the work of God and always goes on to salvation; for what He begins He always finishes. One conviction proceeds from the fear of the punishment and result of sin; the other from the awfulness and the fact of sin. That is the difference. Felix, you remember was convicted. He trembled before Paul, but said, "Go thy way, I'll see you again some other time." He was convicted, he trembled, he probably wept. There was a great emotional disturbance, but as far as we know, nothing happened whatsoever after that. But our Lord Jesus Christ says in chapter 16 of John, verses 8 and 9, concerning the Holy Spirit:

> And when he is come, he will reprove the world of sin, and of righteousness, and of judgment:
> Of sin, because they believe not on me.

We have to recognize that there is a true and a false conviction of sin, and a true and false repentance. Here we have Joe and John, both seem to be pricked in their hearts by the Word of God, and at the invitation both come forward. Both of them get down on their knees, shed tears and seem to be deeply moved. But John happens to be in a bad situation. He would like to get out of it and to escape the penalty which is hovering over him. Joe is thinking of his past life and how he has grieved the Lord. He wants to be saved. He is convicted of sin. John is only sorry that he got caught. If his sin had not been discovered, he would never have come forward or confessed it. Now we deal with both of them. After they have prayed, we send them both away and we put down, "John and Joe."

We do not know whether either of them is saved, and yet we often strut around and say, so many were converted in the meeting. I come back a year later and I say to the pastor of the church, "Do you remember about a year ago in one

of our meetings here two men came forward at the invitation?
How about them? Tell me, how are they getting along?"
He replies, "Well, Dr. De Haan, I am happy to report about
Joe. Joe was born again all right. He was saved. You know,
since that day he has just grown and grown and grown. He
feeds on the Word, does not miss a service, stands on the street
corner and hands out tracts, testifies and leads many people
to Christ. He is a soul-winner and a shining light. Everybody
knows where Joe stands. Yes, Joe was truly converted."
Then the pastor's voice drops, and he says, "But John — I'm
sorry; that's another story. He was all right for about
three or four weeks, and then we began to miss him in the
meetings. After a while he didn't show up at all any more.
When we would try to contact him, he wouldn't have anything to do with us. Today he is back in the world, back in
sin, deeper than he ever was before."

Now God knew all the time that John never was saved
when he came forward. When the storm was past and the
dangers gone, he drifted back to his old life. God saw the
faith in Joe's heart and saved him. But you and I had to
wait until the evidence of his works before we were able to
evaluate the genuineness of his conversion experience. In
fact, God knew it from eternity, but we had to wait until we
saw the evidence. How important, therefore, works become
in regard to our testimony. They are necessary as the evidence
and the assurance of the work of grace and faith which has
already been accomplished in our hearts.

CHAPTER SEVENTEEN

The Practicality of Faith

In the previous chapter we took up the matter of faith and works, concerning which there has been a great deal of confusion among Christian believers. Paul in his Epistle to the Romans very definitely sets down the fact that works have absolutely nothing to do with salvation, that salvation is entirely a matter of faith and faith alone. James, however, tells us that a man is justified not only by faith, but by works as well. Paul writes in Romans 4:1-4:

> What shall we say then that Abraham our father, as pertaining to the flesh, hath found?
>
> For if Abraham were justified by works, he hath whereof to glory; but not before God.
>
> For what saith the scripture? Abraham believed God, and it was counted unto him for righteousness.
>
> Now to him that worketh is the reward not reckoned of grace, but of debt.

When we turn to the Epistle of James we find this (2:21):

> Was not Abraham our father justified by works, when he had offered Isaac his son upon the altar?

We can only understand this apparent contradiction when we remember that Paul is quoting from chapter 15 of Genesis where Abram believed what God had said concerning the promised son, but James takes quite a different incident out of the life of father Abraham. His quotation refers back to chapter 22 of Genesis, to an incident which occurs some forty years after Abraham had been justified by faith. Therefore we read:

> Was not Abraham our father justified by works, when he had
> offered Isaac his son upon the altar?

You will notice that James does not say, "when he offered,"
but "when he *had* offered." It was not until *after* Abraham
had offered up his son, Isaac, that he was justified by works
in the sight of men. Forty years before he had already been
justified by faith in God's sight, but now he is justified by
works before men.

We see, then, that the Bible teaches two kinds of justification, one by faith and another by works. There is no contradiction, but a wonderful, harmonious revelation — in God's
sight, faith; in man's sight, works. Both Paul and James use
father Abraham to illustrate their point but use quite different
incidents from Abraham's life.

CANAANITES AND PERIZZITES IN THE LAND

Abram had come from the Ur of the Chaldees together
with Lot and had settled in the land of Canaan. He came
with an entirely new religion of Jehovah. Undoubtedly the
Canaanites and the Perizzites who were then in the land
looked dubiously upon these two strangers who came from a
far-off land. They probably wondered whether this religion
was real, or just something else again that came and was to
go. I can imagine them saying, as they looked at Abraham
worshipping and serving the Lord, "We'll see, we'll see. We'll
just wait a little while. We'll see how it works out in time."
(You know, there are people who are very skeptical about a
believer's profession.) "If it is like the rest of what we see, it
will only be a little while. Just wait until the test comes
and the trials come; he will soon give up his faith in God
then. This is all fine and good when things are going prosper-
ously, but just wait until the real test shows up." So they
must have waited.

Then the time came when Abraham obeyed God, and took
his son upon the mountain to sacrifice him. We read the
record:

> And it came to pass after these things, that God did tempt
> Abraham, and said unto him, Abraham: and he said, Behold,
> here I am.
> And he said, Take now thy son, thine only son Isaac, whom
> thou lovest, and get thee into the land of Moriah; and offer him
> there for a burnt-offering (Genesis 22:1, 2).

Abraham must now bind his son upon the altar, shed his
blood, put him to death. Both in Hebrews and in James we
are told that Abraham actually, as far as God was concerned,
did sacrifice his son. In both books the phrase "offered
Isaac" is used (Hebrews 11:17, James 2:21).

When the Canaanites saw this, every mouth was stopped.
There was no more criticism, no more doubting, for here was
indisputable evidence of Abraham's faith in God. As he went
up to the mountains to sacrifice his son, I can hear these
people saying, "This thing must be real; this thing is working;
this must be genuine." When a man will go all the way, not
only part of the way, but as far as God leads him; when
he will give up the very thing which is more precious than
life itself, in obedience to God as a testimony; this must be
real. And so I read at the end of the narrative one of the
most precious verses in the Bible:

> Was not Abraham our father justified by works, when he
> had offered Isaac his son upon the altar?

James goes on to say in verse 22 of chapter 2:

> Seest thou how faith wrought with his works, and by works
> was faith made perfect.

"Perfect" means complete. Faith was made complete in this
act of Abraham, in this evidence of faith; "and the Scripture
was fulfilled which saith, Abraham believed God" (James
2:23). The goal of his faith was the evidence of that faith in
works. That is the story of salvation. God's purpose in saving
us is not to keep us out of hell, merely. That is an incidental
thing, although quite necessary in the process. His purpose in
saving us is to make us like Himself. That is what James is

talking about: a little more reality, a little less shouting about our faith, and more demonstration of our real faith in God.

FRIEND OF GOD

Notice the next phrase which ends verse 23:

And he was called the Friend of God.

That's a wonderful statement! When was Abraham called the friend of God? After he had demonstrated the reality of his faith in God. Who called him the friend of God? We believe, personally, that the people round about him called him the friend of God. In Genesis, of course, we are also told that he was called the friend of God by the Lord Himself, but here it seems to indicate that the people who saw this act of faith on the part of Abraham called him God's friend. I personally do not know a thing that I would rather have people say about me before I go home to glory than "that man was a friend of God." Yes, I would be willing to go into His presence just with that one statement.

How are people going to know that we are friends of God? Only by seeing our works. That is the only way. Has there been anything in your conduct and conversation today or in this past week, as you mingled among men in the community, which led them to believe that you are a friend of God? Or did you go to the places the world frequents without even letting them know that you are different by your conversation and by your conduct and by your testimony. One trouble in the church is that there are so many Christians who do nothing wrong, but who neither do anything positive in their life by which the world may know that they are truly children of God. They live good, honest, law-abiding lives, but there is nothing to indicate that they are serving the Lord Jehovah God, and are believers in the Lord Jesus Christ. The trouble with so many believers is that they do not do anything. They do not do this, and they do not do that; they do not commit this sin nor do they commit that sin; but there is nothing else positive in their lives. A man says, "I don't swear, I don't drink, I don't gamble, I don't steal." I say to him, "My friend, what do you do? Do you do anything at all? When you sat down to eat today in the restaurant, did you sit down just as all the rest of the world, or did you let people know that you were a friend of God by asking God's blessing upon that which He had provided for you?"

The world today is waiting for a demonstration of the genuineness and the reality of our faith. It is wondering whether we can stand the test and can meet the greatest crisis in life without murmuring. The world is sick of a lot of preaching, sick and tired of a profession. It needs a demonstration of what God can really do. So James continues, in a striking way:

> What doth it profit, my brethren, though a man *say* he hath faith? (James 2:14).

ACTIVE FAITH NEEDED

Now the emphasis here should be placed on "say." Faith means nothing at all, if it is not backed up by works. James says in effect: "Though a man say he hath faith, and have not works, can that kind of a faith save him?" That is the meaning here and that is the argument. He continues therefore in verse 15:

> If a brother or sister be naked, and destitute of daily food,
> And one of you say unto them, Depart in peace, be ye warmed and filled; notwithstanding ye give them not those things which are needful to the body; what doth it profit?

Do you get the force of this? He says, "Quit talking, and start doing something." I have seen more deviltry covered up by pious praying and pious phrases and testifying than by anything else I know of in the world. One of the worst rascals I ever met used to separate poor widows, and rich widows too, from their possessions by piously calling on them and seeking to comfort them and praying with them, while all the while he was really "preying" upon them. Some of the worst people in the country today are carrying on their pernicious program under the guise of religion and the preaching of the blood of Christ. They are separating men and women from their money by every unscriptural method. May God help us to get down to the reality of these things.

> What doth it profit, my brethren, though a man say he hath faith, and have not works? can faith save him?
>
> If a brother or sister be naked, and destitute of daily food, And one of you say unto them, Depart in peace, be ye warmed and filled; notwithstanding ye give them not those things which are needful to the body; what doth it profit?

James implies that all the time we have in our possession the means whereby to provide that which they need, but instead we still hold it back and try to justify our covetousness by pious prayers and pious phrases. Oh, beloved, we deny the faith if we are able to help a brother or a sister materially in their physical needs, even though it be at our own sacrifice, but merely say instead, "Oh, we're so sorry for you. Yes, it is indeed too bad. We'll pray for you. Shall we pray about this?" Listen, my friends, that brother, that sister, does not need our hypocritical prayers. That is not their need at the present time. They need our help. James, too, is just a bit tired of some of this piety, and says, "If your brother is cold, do something for him." And that is true today. If a brother or sister are poor and are cold, they need a ton of coal, not our prayers. God is not going to answer our prayer to send coal as long as He knows that we have twenty dollars in our pocketbook.

The world today is looking for a definite, practical experience of the reality of our faith. We have so much superficial, shallow preaching. Believe, believe, believe, we tell the world, but the world simply will not believe unless they see the reality of faith in our own lives. The average man has little respect for the Christian who only talks. I think we could even do without a lot of praying, if we would use the time which we have in a more definite and practical way. You may have heard of the captain of the ship who, when the boat was on fire and everybody was carrying water in the bucket brigade, saw a man who was kneeling on the deck and praying very piously to the Lord to put out the fire. The captain came over and shouted in his ear, "This is no time to pray. This is the time to carry water."

Total Commitment

I close, therefore, with the question again, Why did God save us? Just to keep us out of hell? Indeed, not; but thank God that this is included. Why did God save us? Just to take us to heaven when we die? No, but thank God, that too is included. God has saved us for the one distinct purpose of making us like the Lord Jesus (Romans 8:29), so that when men see us they will take note of us and know that we have been with Him. I repeat: Your conduct today, not only what you have said, but what you have done and accomplished as you mingled with people, has been your testimony of your faith in God. Do people know that you are a friend of God? I have known people, and know some now, who are so completely Christlike that when they walk into a place a hush comes over the entire scene. They are known for being friends of God. Oh that God might move upon our hearts so that we might be willing to make a complete and a full and a definite and a final surrender to Him, as Abraham did. Then all of our lives, everything that we are from this day on, would serve to let men and women know that we are Christ's. I want to tell you that if only a small fraction of you who are reading this message would go out tomorrow, all out for God, with the absolute determination to be yielded to Him wholeheartedly, and not let a single opportunity go by of demonstrating and showing to men and women the love of Christ, it would do more good than all the Bible conferences, revival meetings and evangelistic meetings in all the world. We need men and women today who are willing to go all the way as Abraham did.

Oh, the bitter pain and sorrow,
    That a time could ever be,
When my proud heart said to Jesus,
    All of self, and none of Thee.

But He found me; I beheld Him,
    Hanging on the accursed tree,
And my trembling heart then whispered,
    "Some for self, and some for Thee."

But day by day, His tender mercy,
    Wooing, loving, full and free,
Drew me closer, closer, 'till I whispered,
    "Less of self, and more of Thee."

Higher than the highest mountain,
    Deeper than the deepest sea,
Lord, at last thy love has conquered;
    Now it's none of self, and all of Thee.

That is what God expects that we shall do — go all out for Him.

Let your light so shine before men, that they may see your good works, and glorify your Father which is in heaven (Matthew 5:16).

CHAPTER EIGHTEEN

The Two Natures

Now Sarai Abram's wife bare him no children: and she had an handmaid, an Egyptian, whose name was Hagar.

And Sarai said unto Abram, Behold now, the Lord hath restrained me from bearing: I pray thee, go in unto my maid; it may be that I may obtain children by her. And Abram hearkened to the voice of Sarai.

And Sarai Abram's wife took Hagar her maid the Egyptian, after Abram had dwelt ten years in the land of Canaan, and gave her to her husband Abram to be his wife.

And he went in unto Hagar, and she conceived: and when she saw that she had conceived, her mistress was despised in her eyes (Genesis 16:1-4).

There are moments in the life of the father of the faithful, Abram, when one would hardly recognize him as a child of God. In those moments of doubt, when he seems to forget all about his responsibility toward God, he does some of the things which can only remind us of the awful deceitfulness of the flesh which still remains within the believer. And yet God uses some of these experiences as stepping stones for greater victories which lie ahead.

Every believer is predestinated by God according to His Word to become ultimately like the Lord Jesus. This we have pointed out repeatedly in the past chapters as the clear teaching of Romans 8:29. When we see what the Lord has to begin with when He finds the sinner, we see something of the gigantic task which God undertakes. He seeks a poor, good-for-nothing, hell-deserving sinner, in the mire and slime

of sin, and says in effect, "I'm not going to stop working on
him until he is like my own lovely Son, the Lord Jesus
Christ." If God merely saved the sinner to keep him out of
hell, it would be much. If He saved him to keep him out of
hell and also to take him to heaven, it would also be a great
deal. But to make him ultimately like the Lord Jesus is a
tremendous undertaking.

The Testing By God

We can, therefore, understand why God is continually
working on His children. There are few periods in our
lives when we are completely free from some kind of testing,
some kind of trial. God is continually turning over, smoothing
out here and there, until we often wonder why we have so
little peace and tranquillity in this life. It is only because God
is trying to make something out of us, trying to do something with us. He has a purpose in mind. In our study of
the life of Abram, the great example of faith, we find this illustrated over and over again.

First Abram had to leave his kindred and his country, which
was a test of faith, test of separation from those who were
dear to him. Then came the test of providence, whether he
would remain in the land when the famine came. And we
saw how Abram failed and fled to Egypt. Then we saw the
trial of his testimony, whether he would realize that the
Canaanite and the Perizzite were watching him, and whether
he would dare to trust God in the matter of that which he had
received. There came then the test of his courage, whether
he would dare, with just a handful of untrained servants, to
meet the four great kings in faith and show his love for his
nephew. After that there came the test concerning covetousness and the love of the goods of this world, when the king
of Sodom offered him all the spoil. Then there was the test
of the assurance of faith, whether he really would believe God
only on the simple record of His word and the record of Calvary. Now we come to chapter 16 where we have recorded

one of the most severe tests which ever comes into the life of a Christian — the test of patience, whether we are able to believe God enough to wait until He is ready to answer our prayer. The test of patience is a severe test, to be sure. We shall see how miserably Abram failed and thus profit from his sin.

We have read for you the story of how Abram at the suggestion of Sarah took the handmaid, the Egyptian, a slave girl, and raised up a seed by her because he could not wait for the promise of God to be fulfilled. It is indeed difficult to imagine that this is the identical man of faith whom we saw in the preceding chapters of Genesis, who believed God upon the simple testimony of His word and became the example of justifying faith. It is almost inconceivable that the same man who could trust God so implicitly could now, just a little while later, yield to the temptation of impatience and of the flesh, and could commit an act which even in the light of the moral standards of his day was absolutely unjustifiable and wicked in the extreme.

CHANGE OF NAMES

It is hard to understand Abraham's actions unless we recognize the presence of the two natures in every believer. This great man of faith had two names, "Abram," his first name, and his second, God-given name, "Abraham." These names bring us face to face with a tremendous fact. Abraham was the name which God gave to the spiritual man, but Abram was his name by natural birth.

You may recall that Abraham's grandson, Jacob, also had two names. The first, "Jacob," signified the sinner; the second, "Israel," the saint. "Jacob" means crook and cheat. That is what God says the man is by his first birth. He is totally depraved and utterly corrupt; and we are no better than Jacob. "Jacob" comes from an incident which happened at his birth. When Jacob was born he was born a twin. As Esau was being born, the unborn Jacob lay hold of Esau's heel as if to try to keep him from being born. From the fact that he lay hold of the heel of his brother, he was given the name, Jacob; for the name comes from the expression, "the heel-holder," or "the tripper-upper." Before Jacob was even born, he was already trying to trip up his brother, Esau, and that trait became characteristic of his life. What a rascal he was, and what he turned out to be. He cheated his father, connived with his mother, robbed his brother and well-nigh ruined his uncle Laban in Padan-aram. That was Jacob by his first birth. But before God was through with Jacob, He said, "Your name is not going to be Jacob anymore, but your name is going to be Israel." "Israel" comes from three Hebrew words: *Ish,* which means a man; *ra,* which means great; and *El,* which is a fragment of one of the names of God, Elohim. "Ish-ra-el" therefore means the great man, or prince, of God. This was the name that God gave him. Jacob, the crook becomes Israel, the prince of God. But while he was Israel, he was also still Jacob; and while Abram became Abraham, he was also still Abram.

We think of Simon Peter. "Simon" was his name by his first birth; "Peter" was the name Christ gave him, and it represented the second birth. But "Simon" was not eradicated when he became "Peter." When Peter wrote his final epistle, just before he died, the very first two words of that epistle, from the pen of Peter, are "Simon Peter." That is the way he introduces his last message to us. He seems to say by these two words, "Oh, thank God, I am Peter, but I am sorry that old Simon is still with me, even to the end of my life." Peter had to learn his lesson by many painful experiences.

That there are two natures co-existing in man is, I think, the lesson the Lord is trying to teach us in the rather sordid record of Abram's listening to the voice of his wife, Sarai. This record brings us face to face with one of the greatest fundamental truths of the Word of God, the neglect of which

and the ignorance of which is causing so much trouble in
Christian circles.

NEW BIRTH NOT REBIRTH

Everywhere the world around we have confusion concerning the two natures. We must remember that the new
birth is not a rebirth but definitely a new birth. When a
person is born again, God does absolutely nothing to the
old man of the flesh. The old nature is so hopelessly, incor-
rigibly corrupt that even God Himself will not bother to
repair it or salvage it. Instead of doing that, He places within
an individual a brand new nature, eternal and forever separate
from the old.

Every new man becomes two men before Almighty God.
He still is the "old man" and he is also the "new man"; and
these two are incompatible. This, beloved, is the cause of the
conflict in the Christian life. In Genesis 15 we have the new
man in ascendancy as Abram believes God and becomes the
great example of faith. But in the very next chapter, Genesis
16, we have the old man in the ascendancy. The old Adam
here is very evident. Abram could not wait for God to perform His work; He became impatient; he was unwilling to
wait for God to keep His Word; he wondered if God were
really going to fulfill His promise after all. He began to fret
and stew and moan. Finally Sarah said, "Well, I can't live
with you under these conditions. I'd better do something."
So she made the utterly sinful, fleshly suggestion that he raise
up a seed by her handmaid, Hagar.

It is well to remember what our Lord Jesus Christ said in
the third chapter of the Gospel according to John, where we
not only have that great doctrine of the new birth, but also
that of the two natures set forth in a most remarkable way:

> Verily, verily, I say unto thee, Except a man be born again,
> he cannot see the kingdom of God (vs. 3).

Nicodemus did not understand completely what the Lord was
speaking about, so he, supposing that the new birth was a re-

birth of the old nature or a repairing of the old man, answers the Lord in these words:

> How can a man be born when he is old? can he enter a second time into his mother's womb, and be born (vs. 4)?

The reason Nicodemus asked this question was simply that he did not yet understand the fact that the new birth was an entirely new creation on the part of God, and not an altering or a repairing of the old man in any sense of the word. In His answer our Lord Jesus seems to say, "You don't understand thoroughly, Nicodemus, what I am talking about," and so He continues:

> Except a man be born of water and of the Spirit, he cannot enter into the kingdom of God. (vs. 5).

FROM ABOVE

All the difficulty arises from the fact that "again," in the third and seventh verses is translated incorrectly. The word translated "again" is *anothen* and does not mean again but it means *from above*. What Jesus actually says is this: "Verily, verily, I say unto you, Except a man be born *from above*, he cannot see the kingdom of God." When the Lord comes to us, and we trust Him, and the new birth takes place, He does nothing to the old nature whatsoever, but creates a brand new thing. And we can say with Paul:

> Therefore if any man be in Christ, he is a new creature (II Corinthians 5:17).

This does not mean that he is a repaired creation. God does not salvage us, but He saves us when we are born again. He makes an entirely new being. The old is doomed to destruction: It must be ultimately eradicated. Within a saved person dwells that new man which is the divine nature, which is "Christ in you the hope of glory." Thus every saved man becomes two men.

CHAPTER NINETEEN

The Comfort of Faith

And Abram was fourscore and six years old, when Hagar bare Ishmael to Abram (Genesis 16:16).

Genesis 16, which relates the backsliding of Abram, ends with the statement of the age of Abram at the time Ishmael, the son of the flesh, was born. It tells us that he was "fourscore and six," or eighty-six years old when this child of Abram's impatience came into the world. It is significant that the first verse of chapter 17 also begins with a statement as to the age of Abram at the time the Lord again appeared unto him:

And when Abram was ninety years old and nine, the Lord appeared to Abram.

It is important that we notice these figures which the Holy Spirit has purposely placed in these two adjoining verses. First of all, we put down the number, 99, and then subtract 86, the age of Abram at the close of chapter 16. We come to the amazing result of 13. There are exactly thirteen years between the last verse in chapter 16 and the first verse in chapter 17. Here is a period of thirteen years during which nothing is recorded by the Holy Spirit whatsoever in the life of the man of faith, Abram. Thirteen wasted, blasted years. Thirteen years in the flesh. A saint of God, Abram, the father of the faithful and the friend of God, wasted thirteen precious years, without an altar, without a revelation. No covenant, no fellowship, no prayer, no fruit, no growth, no progress, nothing worthy of recording. Abram evidently lived in this sin of Ishmael for thirteen wasted years because he could not wait for God's time, but became impatient and took things into his own hands. Did you ever realize that impatience is also a sin? When we think of fleshly sins we think of adultery, fornication, lasciviousness, worldliness and drunkenness, but impatience is a sin of the flesh also; and evidently a terrible one, for God certainly dealt harshly with Abram here.

God Abides Faithful

Now, however, comes the best part of the entire story: God did not forget His child nor cast him off just because Abram was trying to forget about the promises of the Lord. The Bible definitely tells us in II Timothy 2 that if we "deny him, he will also deny us: if we believe not, yet he abideth faithful: he cannot deny himself." We find that God denied Abram thirteen years of fellowship and blessing, but did not deny His promise; He did not deny Himself. He denied blessing to Abram and He denied him power and He denied him new revelation, but God could not deny Himself, for Abram was still God's child. All of that time God was remembering him. Certainly if God had been as unfaithful as Abram, he would be in hell today; but the Lord said instead, "I will not let you go." After these thirteen long years, God comes to this child once more to restore him to fellowship.

Grace! Oh, what marvelous grace! God would not let his erring child go. All the time God's heart had been bleeding and yearning, but He waited until Abram had thoroughly learned his lesson. Then after thirteen years, God appears to him and says to him: I am the Almighty God (Genesis 17:1). God seems to say to him, "You thought that I couldn't do it. You didn't count on my Almightyness. You became impatient and thought that I had forgotten and that I needed help. You resorted to the flesh, and now, look what you have gotten yourself into."

LET THE SPIRIT LEAD

What a lesson all of this presents to us here. How we too suffer in our personal life and in our church life when we fail to depend upon the leading of the Spirit of God and fail to trust Him for all of our needs, when we begin to resort to the flesh and fleshly methods and means, whether in our financial or other affairs. Then God repeats the barren years of Abram, and these sometimes amount to more than thirteen years in the life of a Christian. How prone we are when the least bit of testing comes to resort to fleshly means. From personal experience I can testify that it has been so in the work of the Radio Bible Class. How often during the last thirteen years the flesh has tempted and suggested that we give God just a little bit of a help in maintaining the broadcasting. There have been periods during this time when our faith was severely tested, when we began to figure in our own fleshly calculation that in a few more weeks we would probably be all through. It was then that the flesh whispered and suggested the use of some carnal, fleshly means and methods of promotion. I am sure, without a shadow of a doubt, that if we had listened to the flesh instead of trusting God, who has kept us going these thirteen years, that He would have done the same thing that He did to Abram.

Brother, sister, you may put this down in your memory book for your church work also: The less of the Spirit of God in the church, the more of fleshly organization you will find; the more of the Spirit of God, the simpler the fellowship and the worship of believers. Let the Spirit have His way, and you will not need fifty-seven different committees for everything which is done in the church of our Lord.

THE GREAT SUSTAINER

God comes to Abram after thirteen years of wasted life, and says:

> I am the Almighty God.

He seems to imply that Abram had forgotten His Almightiness

and His ability to keep His word. This certainly was a tremendous rebuke. "Almighty" is a translation of a beautiful, tender word in the original Hebrew — *El Shaddai,* one of the seven compound names of the Lord. *El* is the word for God, and *Shaddai* is a word which comes from the Hebrew word *shad* and means a woman's breast. So the name, "Almighty God," which God uses here after thirteen years of backsliding, literally means, I am the Breasted God or I am the God with breasts. It is as though God says, "Abram, you are acting like a little baby; you've been saved all these years, and yet you are just an infant. You couldn't depend upon Me or trust Me, but had to take things into your own hands. You haven't made much progress. Listen, Abram, why don't you realize Who I am. I am the Almighty One. Nothing is impossible with Me." So God tenderly invites His child and says, "Come over here, put your weary head upon my breast and rest in my arms. Yield yourself to my love, and be nourished at my own breast." All this is implied in the name, *El Shaddai* — the protector, the nourisher, the nurser, the sustainer. God seems to invite Abram to lay his head upon His bosom, so that instead of drawing strength from the flesh, Abram may suck strength from the only source — the very breast of God. It is one of the most tender pictures in the entire Bible. It is one of the most beautiful pictures of God.

Notice carefully what follows:

> And when Abram was ninety years old and nine, the Lord appeared to Abram, and said unto him, I am the Almighty God; walk before me, and be thou perfect.

God adds this: "Be thou perfect." Now the word for "perfect" means to be complete or mature. God seems to say, "Walk before Me, Abram, and don't get out of my sight again, as you've done. Don't get off the track and listen to Sarah. Walk before Me, and be complete."

> And I will make my covenant between me and thee, and will multiply thee exceedingly.

> And Abram fell on his face: and God talked with him, saying,
>
> As for me, behold, my covenant is with thee, and thou shalt be a father of many nations. (Genesis 17:2-4).

"It is true, Abram, you've been unfaithful, but I will never let you go."

> Neither shall thy name any more be called Abram, but thy name shall be Abraham; for a father of many nations have I made thee (vs. 5).

Before I close this message, I would point out how hard it is to let go of the flesh, how hard to come back again when we have wandered away. In Genesis 17:15-17 we read:

> And God said unto Abraham, As for Sarai thy wife, thou shalt not call her name Sarai, but Sarah [a princess, not a barren old woman] shall her name be.
>
> And I will bless her, and give thee a son also of her: yea, I will bless her, and she shall be a mother of nations; kings of peoples shall be of her.
>
> Then Abraham fell upon his face, and laughed, and said in his heart, Shall a child be born unto him that is an hundred years old? and shall Sarah, that is ninety years old, bear?

Poor Abraham. He had lost all interest in God's promised seed, and so he says in verse 18 a thing that we can hardly imagine coming from the father of the faithful:

> And Abraham said unto God, O that Ishmael might live before thee!

In essence Abraham says, "I've become so attached to the flesh, (Ishmael) I love him so much that I am willing to give up the son of promise." We ask ourselves, Is this possible? Yes, indeed, it is possible to get so deeply into the world and to be so motivated by the flesh that we are willing to give up even our spiritual life for the pleasures of time and sense. But God in grace keeps right on dealing with Abraham.

> Sarah thy wife shall bear thee a son indeed; and thou shalt call his name Isaac [which means laughter]: and I will establish my covenant with him for an everlasting covenant, and with his seed after him (vs. 19).

Skipping over a few chapters to Genesis 21, verse 10, we find God's answer to Abraham's desire that Ishmael might live before him. Here the demand of God to get rid of this son of the flesh comes:

> Wherefore she said unto Abraham, Cast out this bondwoman and her son: for the son of this bondwoman shall not be heir with my son, even with Isaac.

As long as Ishmael was alone in Abraham's tent, everything went along seemingly fine, but when Isaac came there was trouble.

THE STRUGGLE WITHIN

Here is a truth for the Christian believer. When we are born again, we begin to realize what a struggle there is within us. The evidence of really being saved is the fact of the struggle with the flesh, of which we become conscious more than ever after we have been saved. For thirteen years before Isaac, type of the spiritual man, was born, there seems to have been no trouble in Abram's tent, but no sooner is Isaac born than the strife begins. We find also that the people who are really saved are most conscious of their own utter, complete unworthiness. The true test of holiness is this, that the closer we live to God, the more we see our own unworthiness. We can take a sheet from a bed which has been used and is soiled, but if we do not get it close to the light, it may look just as clean as any other. But the closer we take it to the light, the more the soil becomes apparent; and when placed beside a perfectly clean sheet, it will look positively filthy. So too with us. When a man says that he has reached the state of perfection, I would like to put him next to the perfection of the Lord Jesus Christ; for I am sure that he is not living close to the light, but still living in darkness. But if you are having a struggle, believer, if you are conscious of your own weakness, and even fail and you have to cry out. "Oh, God, I am making so little progress, I am having such a battle, such a struggle with my old nature and such difficulty overcoming it," then you have at least a sign of life, and not of death. If there is no struggle at all in the Christian life, it is a sign that there is no life within. And that is not only true of the individual, but even of groups and of churches. May God deliver us from the complacency of death and from a life which has not enough activity even to be conscious of the struggle.

We see struggle in the life of every saint of God, and especially in the life of Abraham. What a struggle it was to gain the victory and give up Ishmael. Hear him, therefore, in Genesis 21:11:

> And the thing was very grievous in Abraham's sight because of his son.

He was not willing as yet to give up Ishmael, and so God comes to him:

> And God said unto Abraham, Let it not be grievous in thy sight because of the lad, and because of thy bondwoman; in all that Sarah hath said unto thee, hearken unto her voice, for in Isaac shall thy seed be called.
>
> And Abraham rose up early in the morning, and took bread, and a bottle of water, and gave it unto Hagar, putting it on her shoulder, and the child, and sent her away (vss. 12, 14).

Thank God, victory at last! He sent her away. He loved Ishmael, but he was of the flesh. There are some things of time and sense and the world which in themselves may not be so very sinful, but they are nevertheless precious to us. God says, "Send them away." Only after Abraham was willing to let go of the flesh did he find victory. And what a victory it was, for the following chapter, Genesis 22, sees Abraham reaching the very pinnacle of victorious faith. You will recall what we have in chapter 22. It is nothing else than the offering of Isaac, the very climax of faith, the victory of faith, when Abraham was willing to put away the flesh and be obedient unto God alone.

Examine Yourself

I would ask the question, Are you walking after the flesh, or after the Spirit? We hear a great deal about sanctification nowadays, and yet few people realize what true Biblical sanctification is. It certainly is not going to the altar or standing on your head, or spinning like a top. It is not "praying through," and it is not "tarrying at the altar." It is not seeing visions, or having icicles going down your back. It is not seeing balls of fire or hearing voices, talking in tongues, or walking on air. Sanctification is a matter of honestly recognizing the presence of the flesh within ourselves, confessing with Paul that in us (in our flesh) "there dwelleth no good thing," frankly judging the old nature and then, by the grace of God, yielding to Him and starving the old nature to death.

Many years ago I heard Dr. Ironside give an illustration which I have never forgotten. He said that he was doing certain work out in the mission among the Indians in New Mexico when an Indian chief was saved at one of the meetings and went back to his tribe. After some weeks he came back, and they asked him at the mission compound, "Chief, how are you getting along since you have been saved?" And he answered, "Well, I have had quite a time. Since I've been saved, I have found out that I have two dogs inside of me, a white dog and a black dog, and they are always fighting and always snapping at each other." And they asked him, "Well, which one of the dogs wins the fight?" And he answered, "Which ever one I say 'sickem' to." That is the answer of the two natures as well. The one that will be in ascendancy is the one which we encourage and feed and pamper and pet. May God grant us the lesson of victory through the example of Abraham.

CHAPTER TWENTY

The Faithfulness of God

> And the Lord visited Sarah as he had said, and the Lord did unto Sarah as he had spoken (Genesis 21:1).

We come in our study of the life of Abraham, the father of the faithful, to the great twenty-first chapter of the Book of Genesis, which records for us the birth of the promised son after many years of delay and many years of impatience on the part of Abraham. God had called Abraham from Ur of the Chaldees, and it is now about thirty years since Abraham had come out of that land. God had made the promise that He would give him a seed and give him a land, and that in the union of this seed and this land would be the blessing of all the world and all the nations. The land and the seed are to be together. At the time God made the promise, Abraham had neither a seed nor did he possess one foot of land. He had to come out entirely by faith. Then for thirty years God kept Abraham waiting, testing his faith, preparing him and working on him in order that in the end He might accomplish the purpose for which He saves all of us, to make us like unto the Lord Jesus Christ.

Verse 1 in Genesis 21 is one of the most important in the chapter and one which has a lesson we would love to drive home to every heart. We quote it again:

> And the Lord visited Sarah as he had said, and the Lord did unto Sarah as he had spoken.

Believers ought to rejoice in this wonderful truth. There is a depth here which is inexhaustible. God would not break

His covenant, even though Abraham had been unfaithful over and over again. He had become impatient, he had become fleshly, he had doubted God, he had quarreled with the Lord, he even went so far as to take matters into his own hands and tried to raise up a substitute for the promised seed in order to help God out of a difficult situation. But the Lord let him go on, for Abraham had to come entirely to the end of himself before he realized that this thing must be left completely in the hands of God. Then we read in verse 2 that God finally did just what He said He was going to do:

> Sarah conceived, and bare Abraham a son in his old age, at the set time of which God had spoken to him.

Now there are many truths right here on the surface which I want you to get. They are commonplace, probably, but they are so tremendously important that we must not pass them by. First of all, we have here the Holy Spirit's declaration concerning the faithfulness of God. We can trust Him, no matter what the circumstances may be; we can trust Him, no matter what the appearances may be, no matter how long the delay; for in God's own good time He is going to keep His Word. He "did unto Sarah as he had spoken."

GOD IS ETERNAL

Notice another thought: God is never in a hurry. That is the great problem with us today. We are so much in a rush and in a hurry, but God is never in a hurry. The Lord is not pressed for time, and we only see this when we realize *Who* He is. God is not a man, He is not limited by time, there is nothing temporal about Him at all. Every one of His attributes are eternal and infinite. God has all eternity to work out His plan and His purpose, which He foreknew and which He foreordained. There was an eternity in the past, before God began the work that He is accomplishing now; for He is the eternal One, and timeless. Our God has no past, He has no future: He lives in the eternal present. Everything that ever was He knew from the beginning. Everything that is ever going to be, He already knows beforehand. He says that even the hairs of our head are numbered, and that not a sparrow can fall to the ground without the will of our Heavenly Father. He calls the stars by name and keeps them in their courses. He knows the vibration of the tiniest atom, and keeps them all in their relationship and in their place. God lives in the eternal present. Everything with Him is *now;* no yesterday; no tomorrow. It is all *now,* because time is a material concept. Before matter was created, there was no time. There could not be any time, for there was no need of time. Time is associated with matter. We have to measure material movements and things in terms of time. Before there was any matter, there could be no time, and so God lives in the eternal present.

When Moses was commanded to go to Israel in the land of Egypt, he asked God what he should say to the children of Israel if they asked him the name of the God of their fathers. And God told Moses to say to the people of Israel, "I AM hath sent me unto you" (Exodus 3:13, 14). Not "I was," not "I'm going to be," but "I am." With God everything is as though it were already done. That is why He was able to say in unfolding His covenant with Abraham, "unto thee have I given this land, and to thy seed after thee," when as yet Abraham did not even have a seed. As far as God was concerned it was as good as accomplished.

QUALITY COUNTS

There is a comforting truth here in this age of rush and hurry and running around. While we are all so restless and out of breath and think that we have to do everything in a hurry, God is not in a hurry. He still takes His time. We wonder why Jesus has not come yet, when we see everything going to pieces. God is not in a hurry and He has still something for us to do.

I do not want to be misunderstood, but I do believe that

we ought to learn this lesson. When I was a young man just starting out in the ministry at the age of about thirty-two, I thought I had to do everything in the first year of my ministry. I acted as though I had to go out and convert the world inside of five years. I thought I had to do the whole thing. There were some severe lessons I had to learn. I have learned that God has His time of doing things, and that He has His ways for doing everything. "Of course," you say, "you're slowing up because you're getting old." That is not true. I am slowing up because I find that God is not in a hurry. Sometimes He wants us to wait for orders before going ahead. God is more interested in being thorough than in doing many things which are shallow and superficial. Today we want mass and bulk and bigness, but God is not particularly interested in them. He is interested in the quality of our work, in the abiding things that really count for God. Jesus said,

> Ye have not chosen me, but I have chosen you, and ordained you, that ye should go and bring forth fruit, and that your fruit should remain. (John 15:16).

After all, it is only that which abides which is of real interest. So God caused Abraham to wait for thirty years, while he, impatient Abraham, resorted to every means and instrument of the flesh in order to help God out; but God was not disturbed by it at all.

AT THE SET TIME

Then thirdly, notice that God does not change His program in order to please us. God had beforehand determined that He would give this son to Abraham when the proper time came:

> Sarah conceived, and bare Abraham a son in his old age, at the set time of which God had spoken to him.

Abraham wanted to hurry this thing up. He says, "That's too long. You're waiting too long, God. It is going to become impossible." But God said, "I have a set time, a predetermined time, and until then I am not going to do anything at all.

In other words, I have a program, and that program includes not only the fact that I will fulfill my promise, but also the steps which will lead up to the preparation for the fulfillment of my promise and the time I am going to do it."

Beloved, there is grave danger today that we shall try to prevail upon God to change His program. The Lord has definitely told us a number of things in His Word; and if you get down and pray contrary to them, your prayers will not be heard. I heard a man sometime ago praying very fervently. "O God stop this war and bring peace upon the earth." Well, I said, that man is wasting his prayer because God said that until Jesus comes and reigns upon this earth, there cannot be peace and there will not be peace. When we pray for peace, and do not mean peace when Jesus comes at His appearing, we are praying contrary to the Word of God. I believe that we have to recognize some of these things, and lest I should be misunderstood, I want to be slow in telling you this. God has told us that things are going to get worse and worse and worse, not better and better and better. Politically, morally, religiously, financially, in every realm, there will be a breakdown of everything that is stable. Our Lord Jesus said:

> When the Son of man cometh, shall he find faith on the earth (Luke 18:8)?

And He told Paul that in the last days perilous times should come, and men should be lovers of themselves and exceedingly wicked (II Timothy 3). In chapter 24 of Matthew, Christ tells us definitely that the end of the age will be with deception, wars, rumors of war, pestilence, earthquakes, famines, intolerance, race hatred, apostasy, and the love of many growing cold. "And this gospel of the kingdom shall be preached in all the world for a witness unto all nations; and then shall the end come."

A world-wide, sweeping revival before the Lord Jesus comes is not in the program of God as far as we can see it. While the expectation of it is born of deep sincerity, it simply is not

the revelation of Scripture. As much as we desire to have it
and would like to pray for it, and God knows we need it, we
find absolutely nothing in the Bible in any way to give any
hope that we will have, this late in the day and before the
Lord comes, a world-wide or even a nation-wide revival.
Rather, we believe that God is going to give local awakenings
and local revivals, we believe God will call out His remnant
and His elect, cement them together and prepare them for
the coming of the Lord Jesus Christ. God has a set time for
everything that He does.

On Schedule

What a comfort to know that God's program goes on
schedule. He has a program in which He takes into con-
sideration every detail. How wonderful! In the morning as we
look ahead into the day about which we know nothing, we
can turn the day over to the One who does know every event
in advance. We know nothing of what is going to happen this
day, nothing of weal or woe, joy or sorrow. We plan, but
how often we do not realize what lies ahead. We do not
know what tragedy will come; we do not know what chal-
lenges will present themselves; we do not know or have any
idea of the temptations which may arise, suddenly, when we
are not prepared. What a joy to say then, each morning,
"Lord we stand before a brand new day. We know nothing
of what lies ahead, not even a minute is known to us, but how
we praise Thee that we can turn to One who does know, who
has planned this day, who knows the trials and the pitfalls and
has given us the promise: 'As thy day, so shall thy strength
be,' and again, 'I will never leave thee, nor forsake thee.'"
That, beloved, is practical Christianity. That is practical faith.

We learn, then, from Genesis 21 that God had a set time.
And when the time came, nothing could stop it. The Lord
came and gave Abraham and Sarah their son, Isaac. Now
as you know, Isaac is a type of the Lord Jesus. In this chapter,
chapter 21, we have the birth of the promised son; then in the

next chapter, 22, we have the death and the resurrection of this promised son. We have in these two chapters the Gospel which was preached before to Abraham. The Gospel of the Lord Jesus is the good news that while we were lost and undone and helpless to save ourselves, God gave His Son to die, to be buried and to rise from the grave for poor lost sinners, so that whosoever believeth on Him should not perish but have everlasting life. Here in chapters 21 and 22 of Genesis is the Gospel presented in a very beautiful, simple way.

LAW OR GRACE

There is another thought: the coming of Isaac meant the going of Ishmael. When Isaac came, Ishmael had to go. Now according to the Epistle of Paul to the Galatians, Sarah and her son, Isaac, correspond to the heavenly Jerusalem. They are the picture of God's grace in keeping His promise and His faithfulness. Paul also tells us that Hagar and her son, Ishmael, type of the flesh, first by natural birth, are typical of Mt. Sinai and of the law. Here, then, the Holy Spirit is revealing that when Jesus Christ comes with His grace, the law age passes. When grace comes, the law of commandments must go, and we enter into a higher relationship, under the new law, which is the law of God's wonderful grace, the law of liberty. We read in Galatians 4:30:

> Cast out the bondwoman and her son: for the son of the bondwoman shall not be heir with the son of the freewoman.

This is, of course, the quotation from the record in Genesis. God seems to say, "No mixing of law and grace. Isaac and Ishmael cannot live in the same tent. No compromise." We hear a great many people talk about law *and* grace, but the truth is law *or* grace. It is one or the other. That Ishmael, who represented the law, had to be cast out at the coming of Isaac, who represented grace, was very grievous in the sight of Abraham; but in Genesis 21:12, we read:

> And God said unto Abraham, Let it not be grievous in thy

sight because of the lad, and because of thy bondwoman; in all
that Sarah hath said unto thee, hearken unto her voice; for in
Isaac shall thy seed be called.

Abraham now comes to the place where he is in the liberty
of grace. I am not a bit surprised that in the next chapter, at
the sacrifice, the climax of Abraham's faith comes; for he was
not ready for it until this particular time. We must realize the
great truth that we under grace are not under the law. Paul
says, "We are free from the law." Ishmael and Isaac cannot
live together in the same house. Ishmael must go. Abraham
was not ready for the climax in his believer's experience, not
ready for the acme, the very victory of faith until he had been
absolutely set free from the works of the law, and was walking
by faith and grace alone, safe in the promises of God. He
had to abandon all confidence in the flesh and his own merit
and his own work, and all hope in the law, before he was
ready to become the example of the father of the faithful and
to merit the wonderful name, the friend of God.

CHAPTER TWENTY-ONE

The Climax of Faith

> And it came to pass after these things, that God did tempt Abraham, and said unto him, Abraham: and he said, Behold, here I am.
>
> And he said, Take now thy son, thine only son Isaac, whom thou lovest, and get thee into the land of Moriah; and offer him there for a burnt offering upon one of the mountains which I will tell thee of (Genesis 22:1, 2).

In this chapter we come to the very climax, the acme and the goal of the faith of Abraham. When God called this man, He had this climax in mind and was looking forward to this record in chapter 22 of Genesis. It took the Lord sixty years to prepare Abraham for this climactic event. The Lord never does put us to the test until we are ready for it. He never sends a trial or a test, except He has made preparation for us to come through victorious. Paul says in I Corinthians 1:13:

> There hath no temptation taken you but such as is common to man: but God is faithful, who will not suffer you to be tempted above that ye are able; but will with the temptation also make a way to escape, that ye may be able to bear it.

What a tremendous comfort this is to us! If God had asked Abraham to sacrifice his son before this time, he would not have been ready for it. So God waited for over sixty years, while He passed Abraham through the fires of trial after trial, until Abraham was finally ready to gain the victory and to earn the names, the father of the faithful and the friend of God.

Thus far we have traced Abraham's journey from Ur of the Chaldees into a land which he had never seen and which he accepted by faith. He was seventy years old when he left Ur of the Chaldees; now he is almost an hundred and thirty years old. In Genesis 12 we have the beginning of the journey of faith; in Genesis 22 we have the climax of this life of faith — the sacrifice of his only, beloved son, Isaac. For sixty long years it had been a tedious and a difficult journey for Abraham. It had been one test and one temptation after another, each one making him just a bit stronger. Sometimes he did go down; at other times he had the victory. But each experience in the overruling providence of God was preparing him for this final victory in chapter 22. Every single thing which happened in his life had for its goal this ultimate victory. God saw beforehand the purpose in Abraham's life for which He had called him, and moved on to that end with unerring persistence. The purpose was finally to conform Abraham unto the image of God. Everything that happened had some bearing, somewhere along the line, on this final victory. What a commentary on Romans 8:28 is the history of Abraham:

> And we know that all things work together for good to them that love God, to them who are the called according to his purpose.

Again I remind you that God is never in a hurry. He took sixty long years to accomplish that which He began when He called Abraham as a Gentile out of the Chaldean land. But remember also that God would not place the great test upon him until he was absolutely ready for it. He would not ask him to do this thing which climaxed the whole life of faith until He had thoroughly prepared and steeled Abraham. I have repeated and emphasized this fact, for I know that we all need this lesson in our own lives. God is also dealing with us in the same way. The road is rough sometimes, there is famine and sometimes there is thirst and temptation and trial and testing until we cry out to God in our distress. But through it all, He assures us that everything which happens to us is for that one great purpose, to conform us to the image of Christ:

> For whom he did foreknow, he also did predestinate to be conformed to the image of his Son, that he might be the first-born among many brethren (Romans 8:29).

In the life of Abraham, this purpose of God finds its climax in the sacrifice of Isaac. God had been causing everything to work together. In His foreknowledge He had purposed, that before He got through with Abraham, Abraham would become a picture of God's own sacrificing love in giving His own Son.

READY AT LAST

The story as we have it in that remarkable twenty-second chapter of Genesis begins as follows:

> And it came to pass after these things.

I would have you stop here just a moment to notice that it says, "it came to pass *after* these things." It did not come to pass *before* these things, or *during* these things, for Abraham then could not have stood it. He would have gone down again, for he was not yet prepared. It came to pass *after* these things "that God did tempt Abraham." It was only after all the things recorded in these chapters from Genesis 12 to 21. Now the word "tempt," as used here means to try or to test. God was giving Abraham the final, acid test.

Verse 1 continues:

> And [God] said unto him, Abraham: and he said, Behold, here I am.

Abraham is ready at last. There is no quibbling, no repining now; no arguing any more; no asking questions this time. Abraham did not say now, "O that Ishmael might live before thee." He has finally become a completely submissive wholly yielded and totally prepared vessel at the feet of God. That is the meaning of, "Behold, here I am."

God then says, verse 2:

> Take now thy son, thine only son Isaac, whom thou lovest,
> and get thee into the land of Moriah.

In the original Hebrew the language is far more tender than
this. It should read this way: "And he said, Take now thy
son, thine only Isaac." The word "son" is omitted, and so
the passage reads, "thine only Isaac, whom thou lovest."

Somehow we approach this scene with fear and trembling,
and we feel as though we can hear God saying to us what
He said to Moses on the backside of the desert, "Take off
thy shoes, for the ground whereon thou standest is holy
ground." Nowhere in all the realm of Scripture will we find
a more wonderful, clearer picture of Calvary than in this
chapter. Together with Psalm 22, which is an elaboration of
this chapter, and Isaiah 53, it gives us the most wonderful prophetic picture of the love of God fulfilled at Calvary, when He gave His Son, Jesus Christ. There are so many
beautiful types and shadows here that it is quite impossible
to exhaust this chapter, even in eternity. But I do want to
call your attention to a few of the most outstanding points in
this wonderful narrative. I trust that you will be able to fill
in and add a great many more.

A WILLING FATHER

First of all, then, we have a picture here of the Father's
willingness to give His only Son. God came to Abraham and
said:

> Take now thy son, thine only son Isaac . . . and offer
> him . . . for a burnt offering upon one of the mountains which
> I will tell thee of.

In the entire chapter there is not one single indication of
murmuring, not one sign of repining, not a single word of dis-
content. As far as the record goes, Abraham believed God in
all the fullness of mature faith, and without a single doubt in
his mind was willing to make the supreme sacrifice, to take
his son and to slay him upon the altar, in order that he might

please Him who called him from darkness into light. What a marvelous picture of our Heavenly Father who is foreshadowed in all of these things. Immediately we are reminded of John 3:16:

> For God so loved the world, that he gave his only begotten Son, that whosoever believeth in him should not perish, but have everlasting life.

Isaiah 53:10 goes even farther. There we read these remarkable words:

> Yet it pleased the Lord to bruise him; he hath put him to grief.

We cannot understand the statement that "it pleased the Lord to bruise him." God's love for a poor, lost, hell-deserving sinner was so great that it gave Him pleasure to give His only, well-beloved, spotless Son to save such wretches as we are. Of course we cannot understand this. It goes beyond all human reason. We cannot enter into it all. We can only stand in awe and worship and say, "My Lord, and my God." That is the first thing which is right on the surface here. We see a picture of a loving Father's offering of his Son.

THE ONLY SON

A second beautiful thought is that Isaac is called Abraham's *only* son. What does God mean, "thine *only* son"? Abraham had other sons. He had an Ishmael who was born thirteen years prior to Isaac. He had many sons afterwards, besides those that were born of his servants in the house. God however, recognized as a fit sacrifice only one son, the miraculously born, supernaturally given, promised son. He would not have anything to do with Ishmael, He would not have anything to do with the servants who were born in Abraham's own house, or any of the children that were still to be born by Abraham's future marriage. Isaac is the only one whom God will recognize, and all the blessing that will come upon the rest of the children must come through this one particular son.

God the Father also gave His only Son, but He, too, had many other sons. We read in the Book of Job about a great host of angelic beings called the sons of God. Then, too, Adam is called by Luke a son of God. And we by our new creation are the sons of God. But angels could not fill the requirement for the substitute, and Adam could not pay for his own sin, and we as men were unable to meet God's requirement. There was only One, God's only Son, who was fit to become the substitute for our sin.

THE WELL-BELOVED SON

A third fact that we should notice about Isaac in this verse is that he was Abraham's well-beloved son. How that does warm our hearts, as we think of what God did and said concerning His Son. God says, "Take now thy son, thine only Isaac, whom thou lovest." Notice that: *whom thou lovest!* God, too, had a well-beloved Son. We know as parents something of what the love of a parent is for a child. We would give our very lives, we would lay them down gladly for these precious ones who share our nature. Yet, beloved, our love for our dear ones is so low, so weak, so shallow compared with the love which God had for His Son that all comparisons fade away. It was hard for Abraham to give his well-beloved son. How much more difficult it must have been for God Almighty to give His. For Abraham gave his son out of his love for God, but God gave His Son out of love for His enemies. That love goes beyond all human comprehension.

Jesus said while He was here upon the earth:

> Greater love hath no man than this, that a man lay down his life for his friends (John 15:13).

That is the acme of human love. That is as high as human love can go. This we can somewhat understand. But a love that would die for an enemy who seeks to kill you and hates you — that is a different thing. That indeed is divine love. We are not being taught that kind of love today in the world. We are taught to kill our enemies and to hate those who threaten us so that we may protect ourselves. The love of God as seen in Abraham's example infinitely transcends all love of man; for the love of God as seen in Abraham's example is that he gave his well-beloved son. That is the love that transcends all our understanding.

MOUNT OF THE LORD

We notice next where Abraham is told to go:

> And get thee into the land of Moriah; and offer him there for a burnt offering upon one of the mountains which I will tell thee of (vs. 2).

God pointed out a definite mountain to Abraham in the land of Moriah. Practically all commentaries and Bible students are agreed that the land of Moriah embraced the land of Palestine, and that where Abraham was told to go was Mt. Calvary, the very same mountain on which our Lord was to be crucified. The distance and the time involved correspond exactly to the distance he was to travel and the time consumed in his going there with his son Isaac. But the most conclusive proof of all you will find in the fourteenth verse of this chapter:

> And Abraham called the name of that place Jehovah-jireh: as it is said to this day, In the *mount of the Lord* it shall be seen.

This was a prophetic statement. Abraham says that what transpired in this chapter will be consummated and fulfilled by and by when the real Isaac, the real beloved Son, the real Son of God, will hang upon this same mountain, on Mt. Calvary, in the land of Moriah. Wonderful, marvelous picture the Holy Spirit gives to us all these years before the Lord Jesus Himself came.

EARLY IN THE MORNING

Next we find that Abraham and Isaac began their terrible journey, which must have torn the very heart of Abraham out of his bosom, "early in the morning" (vs. 3). We hope that I am not reading too much between the lines here when we tell you that this undoubtedly points to the arrest and trial of our Lord, early that Wednesday morning of His crucifixion, after the evening in the passover chamber. Then came Gethsemane where they took Him, like a thief and like a robber, and led Him from one judgment hall after another until in the afternoon at three the journey had ended and He cried out, "It is finished." The events began early in the morning.

BEARING THE WOOD

The last picture we call your attention to here is found in verse 6:

> Abraham took the wood of the burnt offering, and laid it upon Isaac his son.

Isaac carried the wood on which he was to die to the place of sacrifice. This certainly is an unmistakable picture of Jesus bearing His Cross as He went to the place called Calvary, bowed down, stooped down, carrying a tree on which He Himself was to die. And while men laid the cross of wood, the symbol of a curse, upon Jesus' shoulder, God placed the curse of sin upon Him. The type becomes complete as Abraham places the wood, the type of the curse, upon the back of his son.

May I appeal to those of you who are still without the Lord Jesus Christ to realize that our Saviour, as He hung on the Cross of Calvary, bore your sin and died for you that you might live. There is only one sin that can condemn you, and that is the sin of rejecting the Lord Jesus Christ, whom God has offered to you in the Person of His Son. Yes, there is only one sin that condemns the sinner today. It is not the degree of sin, but the fact that you have refused God's remedy. The sacrifice now is complete, and He says, "Whosoever will, let him come, and take of the water of life freely."

CHAPTER TWENTY-TWO

Christ in Genesis

> And Abraham took the wood of the burnt offering, and laid it upon Isaac his son; and he took the fire in his hand, and a knife; and they went both of them together.
> And Isaac spake unto Abraham his father, and said, My father: and he said, Here am I, my son. And he said, Behold the fire and the wood: but where is the lamb for a burnt offering?
> And Abraham said, My son, God will provide himself a lamb for a burnt offering: so they went both of them together (Genesis 22:6-8).

Chapter 22 of Genesis presents one of the most dramatic scenes in the entire Scriptures. Unbelief rails and makes fun of it, yet to the Christian believer it is one of the most wonderful and touching scenes of the love of God in all the Bible. Abraham, the father of the faithful, is now ready to sacrifice his only son.

We take up the narrative again as it begins in verse 6 of Genesis 22. Here we have Abraham laying the wood upon the shoulders of his son Isaac. There must have been a great deal of wood, and it must have been a heavy burden. To sacrifice the body of a grown-up man, such as we believe Isaac was, must have taken a great deal of wood. We like to believe that Isaac was as old as the Lord Jesus Christ was at the time of His death. Then Isaac as a type of Christ becomes complete in almost every detail.

The Fire and the Wood

While Isaac carried the wood, Abraham carried the fire which would kindle the wood and cause the sacrifice to be consumed. The wood that Isaac carried points, of course, to the Cross of Calvary. Fire in the Scripture has the meaning of judgment. Again and again fire and flame speak of judgment in preparation for the love of God. It was a flame and a sword that guarded Eden. It was fire which destroyed Sodom and Gomorrah, and very significantly the place of eternal judgment is called the lake of fire. We have here then a picture of the Cross and the judgment which was to fall upon another Son because of the sin of humanity. But that is not all, for we read further in verse 6: "and he took the fire in his hand, *and a knife.*" A knife in Scripture speaks of the Word of God. "The word of God is quick, and powerful, and sharper than any twoedged sword, piercing even to the dividing asunder of soul and spirit, and of the joints and marrow" (Hebrews 4:12).

The great truth is that all of this was according to God's promise and Word. Everything was according to that which He had spoken and according to His plan. Nor was Calvary an after-thought with God. God did not create man, expecting that he would walk in intimacy and fellowship with Him forever. God foreknew and foresaw that man would sin. Even before man was created, God had ready a plan of salvation which included the death of His Son. John in Revelation tells us that Jesus is the "lamb slain from before the foundation of the world." He came in the fulness of time, according to the promise and according to the Word of Almighty God, with a knife in His hand.

Perfect Agreement

Another thing to notice is that "they went both of them together." Here we have perfect agreement. Abraham did not have to force his son to climb up on the altar. They were both agreed and of one mind, and so we read in verse 9:

> And they came to the place which God had told him of; and
> Abraham built an altar there, and laid the wood in order, and
> bound Isaac his son, and laid him on the altar upon the wood.

There is no struggle, no murmuring, no objection. It is the
picture of the son obedient unto death. Here is a man a
hundred and thirty years old, and here is a strapping young
fellow, his son. The old man ties the young man, in the prime
of life, hand and foot, and places him upon the altar without
one word of protest from the son. How well Isaiah has com-
mented on this in Isaiah 53:7 where he speaks of Him of
whom Isaac is the type:

> He is brought as a lamb to the slaughter, and as a sheep
> before her shearers is dumb, so he openeth not his mouth.

Perfect obedience! There was the same agreement between
God and His Son, Jesus.

GOD PROVIDES HIMSELF

Notice, too, what prompted the faith in Abraham's heart.
We read in verse 7:

> And Isaac spake unto Abraham his father, and said, My
> father: and he said, Here am I, my son. And he said, Behold
> the fire and the wood: but where is the lamb for a burnt
> offering?

Isaac was familiar with sacrifice. He knew what its purpose
was, and he asked, therefore, where the lamb for the burnt
offering was. Abraham then gives the most remarkable answer
of faith:

> And Abraham said, My son, God will provide himself a lamb
> for a burnt offering: so they went both of them together (vs. 8).

What did Abraham mean when he said, "God will provide
himself a sacrifice"? Did he mean that God would provide a
substitute, a ram in the bushes? No, Abraham did not know
anything about that. Did he mean that God would provide
something else so that Isaac would not have to die? No, he
did not mean that either. Abraham believed implicitly that
he would have to kill Isaac, actually, and pour out his blood
and burn up his body. But he saw the prophetic meaning of

it all, and he said, "God will provide *Himself*." *He Himself* is going to pay the price. Rather, He Himself is going to be the lamb in the person of His Son. What a marvelous truth of the atonement! When no one else could pay, God said, "I'll pay the price." And that answer satisfied Isaac. He seems to say, "All right, father. That's enough. God will provide Himself a sacrifice for me, if I submit now." "So they went both of them together."

ALONE WITH HIS SON

Now for a moment look at the preparation:

> And they came to the place which God had told him of; and Abraham built an altar there, and laid the wood in order, and bound Isaac his son, and laid him on the altar upon the wood (vs. 9).

When they had reached the top of the mountain, there was nobody but Abraham and Isaac. When they started out from home, a three days' journey back, two men, two servants, had gone along, but when they came to the place where the actual transaction was to take place, Abraham and Isaac were all alone. The transaction was something not for human eyes to behold. We read in verse 5:

> And Abraham said unto his young men, Abide ye here with the ass; and I and the lad will go yonder.

Here is the point that we want to drive home. When they went to the place of sacrifice, they took two men along; but when they came to the mountain, Abraham said, "You two stay behind. I and the lad will take care of the rest of it." When the awful moment for the transaction came, and Abraham lifted up his glittering sword to plunge it in the heart of his only son, there was no one around, no one to witness it, no one to see it. The scene was too sacred, too holy.

Do you see the picture, my friend? When the Son of God went up to Calvary, His Father went with Him, and was right there at Calvary, holding His Son's hand as He walked up the mountain. But there were two other men also,

one on the right hand, and one on the left hand. Then the
time came for the sacrifice, the time for that holy scene which
no eye might behold. Just as Abraham denied the two men
who went with them an opportunity to see the actual transaction, so also did God. For when the time came, every one
must be shut out, and no one must see. From the sixth hour
"there was darkness over the whole earth until the ninth
hour"; for three hours no human eye beheld what took place
on the Cross of Calvary. The Father snuffed out the lights
of heaven, He pulled down the shades of the sky, separated
Himself with His Son alone.

I have often wondered what they must have talked about.
I wonder what they said. Maybe some day we shall know.
Anyway, at the end of those three black hours we hear a cry,
as the Father seems to say to His Son, "I've got to go now.
The rest of the way you will have to go all alone by yourself.
All alone." And there comes the piercing cry from the Son
of God upon the Cross, "My God, My God, why hast Thou
forsaken Me?" Alone He had to die and pay the price, so
that you and I would never have to be alone, so that we would
never have to experience the loneliness of being forever forsaken.

Oh, as we think of this our heart truly is broken. Everyone had forsaken Him; no one was left. Last of all, God hid
His face from His own Son. My heart just melts with grati-
tude when I realize that it was for me that Jesus died on
Calvary's cruel tree; it was for me that Jesus cried, "My God,
why hast Thou forsaken Me?" I want to tell you, my friend,
if you are a child of God, and if that does not melt your heart
to the point of complete dedication to Him, there is something radically wrong. If you are a sinner without Christ, and
that does not melt your heart to say, "My Lord and my God,"
you only deserve the condemnation which you shall receive.
We say it firmly but tenderly because it is true. To reject such

love is worthy of that infinite separation which the Son of God felt Himself as He hung upon the Cross of Calvary.

ISAAC'S DEATH AND RESURRECTION

And then He died. How long was Isaac dead? Three days Yes, exactly three days. That is correct from the record of Scripture. God says that Isaac died. In Hebrews 11, verse 17, we read this:

> By faith Abraham, when he was tried, offered up Isaac.

And the next part says:

> And he that received the promises offered up his only begotten son.

Abraham actually offered up his son in the sight of God. It only means this, that as far as Abraham was concerned, Isaac was really dead. When Abraham started out on the journey early on that morning, he had no other idea than that God meant what He said and that he must after three days put Isaac to death on Mt. Moriah. For three days he considered his son, Isaac, dead, potentially dead. So Isaac becomes a wonderful type of the Lord Jesus Christ in His death, for three days and three nights. Then follows the resurrection.

In Genesis 22, verse 13, we read:

> And Abraham lifted up his eyes, and looked, and behold behind him a ram caught in a thicket by his horns: and Abraham went and took the ram, and offered him up for a burnt offering in the stead of his son.

Isaac had been dead in the mind of Abraham for three days, and now all of a sudden he is returned to life. That is resurrection. Isaac had been considered dead for three days, but now God says, "Take the ram, and let Isaac live." That is resurrection. When we turn to Hebrews 11:17-19 we read this:

> By faith Abraham, when he was tried, offered up Isaac: and he that had received the promises offered up his only begotten son,

> Of whom it was said, That in Isaac shall thy seed be called:
> Accounting that God was able to raise him up, even from the
> dead; from whence also he received him in a figure.

Abraham knew and believed all the time that God was going to do something miraculous. He knew God had promised that Isaac would be the father of the covenant nation, but now he was to die. How then, can God keep His promise? There was only one way out. God, in order to keep His promise, would have to raise up Isaac from the dead. That is all. There was only one way for God to keep His Word under these circumstances, and that was to raise him up again. After three days he was raised up from the dead in type and in figure, and the joy of resurrection was seen upon the mountain where the Son of God was to be slain.

ONLY ONE WAY

Abraham believed in the death and the resurrection of his son. That is the Gospel, and undoubtedly that is what Paul referred to when he says "that the gospel was before preached unto Abraham." Abraham believed it, and because he believed it, he became and was a child of God. My friend, do you realize that this is still the only plan of salvation, the only way that men and women can be saved? They can be saved only through faith in the death and resurrection of the Lord Jesus Christ. This is the message of the Gospel. No matter how great a sinner you are, no matter how far you have gone down in your own sin and degradation, the moment you are willing to put your trust and faith in Him who died and rose to save you, you become like Abraham, a child of God. The Scripture definitely tells you:

> That if thou shalt confess with thy mouth the Lord Jesus,
> and shalt believe in thine heart that God hath raised him from
> the dead, thou shalt be saved (Romans 10:9).

God help you to make that decision now.

CHAPTER TWENTY-THREE

The Gospel of Abraham

> And Abraham stretched forth his hand, and took the knife to slay his son.
>
> And the angel of the Lord called unto him out of heaven, and said, Abraham, Abraham: and he said, Here am I.
>
> And he said, Lay not thine hand upon the lad, neither do thou any thing unto him: for now I know that thou fearest God, seeing thou hast not withheld thy son, thine only son from me.
>
> And Abraham lifted up his eyes, and looked, and behold behind him a ram caught in a thicket by his horns: and Abraham went and took the ram, and offered him up for a burnt offering in the stead of his son.
>
> And Abraham called the name of that place Jehovah-jireh: as it is said to this day, In the mount of the Lord it shall be seen (Genesis 22:10-14).

One of the greatest stumbling blocks in the Scriptures for the unregenerate mind has been the record of Genesis 22 where Abraham is commanded to kill his own son, Isaac, and sacrifice him upon an altar. But to the believer in Christ it is the most marvelous, thrilling story of the love of God. Isaac was spared to be sure, when Abraham his father was about ready to plunge the knife into his bosom; for Isaac was only a type of Jesus Christ, God's Son, and could not fully represent our precious Lord. Isaac himself was a sinner, and needed a substitute. God therefore provided the ram for him in the bushes. The story is an example of a double type in Scripture. Isaac is a type of the Lord Jesus Christ up to a certain point, and then the ram takes his place and becomes God's provision for the sinner.

Abraham understood all the meaning of these things. We hear Jesus saying in John 8:56

> Your father Abraham rejoiced to see my day: and he saw it, and was glad.

Abraham saw in this whole transaction the greater Son, Jesus Himself, and this and this alone can explain his willingness to sacrifice his son without a single objection. Abraham believed that he would actually have to kill Isaac, but he also believed that God would then raise him, as He did Jesus, from the dead. This is definite and clear from verse 5 where Abraham declares that he and Isaac would both come back again, and it is definite from the statement of the author of Hebrews who tells us that Abraham believed God would resurrect Isaac from the dead again. That Abraham already saw in all this a picture of Calvary is made sure by verse 14 of Genesis 22:

> And Abraham called the name of that place Jehovah-jireh: as it is said to this day, In the mount of the Lord it shall be seen.

Abraham says here in effect that the death and resurrection of his son points forward to something greater, the death and the resurrection of the Son of God. That is the unmistakable meaning of the words, "In the mount of the Lord *it shall be seen.*" That is, the fulfillment of all this is still in the future.

THE ASCENSION OF ISAAC

Now comes the most wonderful type of all. After Jesus arose, God's covenant of grace is confirmed and fulfilled. Forty days He spent with His disciples, speaking of the coming kingdom and the blessing of the future. Then He ascended, but not until he had said to them:

> Ye shall receive power, after that the Holy Ghost is come upon you: and ye shall be witnesses unto me both in Jerusalem,

and in all Judaea, and in Samaria, and unto the uttermost part of the earth (Acts 1:8).

There follows the day of Pentecost, and the coming of the Holy Spirit. The nation of Israel is set aside, and passes out of the picture. While Israel has been set aside, the Holy Spirit now is gathering out a Bride for the Son, Jesus. At the end of this dispensation He brings the Bride, the Body of Christ, the church, to come home to be wedded to the Son of God.

You may ask, What has all this to do with Abraham and Isaac? Notice the order of events. First, after Isaac's death and resurrection, God confirms the covenant of grace with Abraham. In Genesis 22:15 — 18 we read:

> And the angel of the Lord called unto Abraham out of heaven the second time,
>
> And said, By myself have I sworn, saith the Lord . . .
>
> That in blessing I will bless thee, and in multiplying I will multiply thy seed as the stars of the heaven, and as the sand which is upon the sea shore . . .
>
> And in thy seed shall all the nations of the earth be blessed.

After the resurrection, the covenant is confirmed, and God promises in addition to the physical seed, Israel, a "starry seed," the church, as well. After Jesus had spent forty days talking to His disciples about the coming kingdom, He too disappears to the mountain and ascends to heaven. This happened to Isaac, the type, as well. Isaac did not come down from Mt. Moriah with his father Abraham, but disappears entirely from this record. Now, of course, we do know that Isaac came down, but as far as the record goes, and the type of Isaac goes, he disappears from view and does not come into the picture until the end of Genesis 24, where Eliezer, the servant, type of the Holy Spirit, comes home with a bride. Notice very carefully the statement of Scripture in Genesis 22:19:

> So Abraham returned unto his young men, and they rose up and went together to Beer-sheba.

It does not say that Isaac returned with them. Isaac disappears from the records, and never appears in this record again until he meets his bride in Genesis 24:62.

What a tremendous picture of the ascension of our Lord Jesus Christ. As Isaac disappears after his resurrection, so Jesus also does. And just as the work is now carried on by Eliezer, the servant sent by the father to call out a bride for the son, so during Jesus' absence the Holy Spirit sent by the Father is calling out His Bride today from among all nations.

PICTURE OF GOD'S PROGRAM

Nowhere in the Scriptures do we find a more beautiful picture of God's program which began at the birth of the Lord Jesus Christ. Follow it closely and your heart will be thrilled, I am sure. In Genesis 21 we have the birth of the promised son. Isaac is supernaturally, miraculously born against the very laws of nature. In Genesis 22 we have the death of this son on Mt. Moriah and Calvary. In the close of this chapter we have the resurrection of this son, Isaac, and then follows his ascension in type as he disappears from view entirely. Notice what happens immediately in Genesis 23. It is the account of the death of Sarah, the mother of the son. Truly, here is a clear type of the setting aside of the nation of Israel after the death and the resurrection of the Son of God, the great antitype of Isaac. We read in Genesis 23, verse 2:

> And Sarah died in Kirjath-arba.

The woman who gave birth to Isaac passes out of the picture. Now in Revelation 12, verses 1,2 and 5, we read of this woman again

> And there appeared a great wonder in heaven; a woman clothed with the sun, and the moon under her feet, and upon her head a crown of twelve stars:
>
> And she being with child cried, travailing in birth, and pained to be delivered.

> And she brought forth a man child, who was to rule all
> nations with a rod of iron: and her child was caught up unto
> God, and to his throne.

Here is a retrospective picture of the woman, the nation of
Israel, bringing forth the man child, who was to rule all
nations with a rod of iron. This child is definitely identified
by David in Psalm 2 as the Lord Jesus Christ. The woman
is Israel, driven into the wilderness of the nations after the
coming of the Son.

COMPLETION OF THE PICTURE

So the picture becomes complete and clear. Sarah dies,
the woman who gave birth to the son is set aside, buried
among the nations, scattered, while the Bride is being called
out, *until* the fullness of the Gentiles be come in. Sarah is
dead, and now Abraham sends his servant, Eliezer, to a
far country to seek a bride for the son, Isaac. It is a long and
tedious journey. When he returns, Isaac comes out to meet
Rebekah in the field, and takes her into his mother Sarah's
tent. This points to the rapture of the church when the Bride
is finally brought home. We shall discuss this matter further in
coming chapters.

After Sarah's death, Abraham remarries:

> Then again Abraham took a wife, and her name was Ke-
> turah.
> And she bare him Zimran, and Jokshan, and Medan, and
> Midian, and Ishbak, and Shuah (Genesis 25:1, 2).

Abraham remarries and becomes the father of six sons, and an
unrecorded number of daughters. Here, then, we have the
future blessing of all the nations through the seed of Abraham,
and God's covenant promise is finally fulfilled. After the
death and the resurrection of Isaac, the death of Sarah, the
calling of the bride, comes the blessing of Abraham and the
birth of all these children. Surely the lesson is clear.

After the death and the resurrection of the Lord Jesus
Christ, the nation of Israel was also set aside, and the Holy
Spirit of Pentecost came upon the scene. The Bride is being

called out. Soon will be the meeting of the Bridegroom, and the wedding in the sky, to be followed by the glorious, millennial, Messianic Kingdom, when all nations shall be blessed through the seed of Abraham. This day certainly cannot be far off. Most of the prophecy of the type of Abraham is already history by this time. The Son has come, He has been born, He has been sacrificed, He has arisen, and He has ascended, and is today at the right hand of the Majesty on high. The Holy Spirit too has come, and the bride is being called out. Soon we shall see our Isaac as He comes to meet us. Then the blessing of the kingdom on this earth shall be fulfilled when,

> Jesus shall reign where'er the sun
>   Doth his successive journeys run;
> His kingdom stretch from shore to shore,
>   Till moons shall wax and wane no more.

Then shall the words of Isaiah be fulfilled as God gave them thousands of years ago, Isaiah 2:2-4:

> And it shall come to pass in the last days, that the mountain of the Lord's house shall be established in the top of the mountains, and shall be exalted above the hills; and all nations shall flow unto it.
>
> And many people shall go and say, Come ye, and let us go up to the mountain of the Lord, to the house of the God of Jacob; and he will teach us his ways, and we will walk in his paths: for out of Zion shall go forth the law, and the word of the Lord from Jerusalem.
>
> And he shall judge among the nations, and shall rebuke many people: and they shall beat their swords into plowshares, and their spears into pruninghooks: nation shall not lift up sword against nation, neither shall they learn war any more.

CHAPTER TWENTY-FOUR

The Holy Spirit and Abraham

> And Abraham was old: and well stricken in age: and the Lord had blessed Abraham in all things.
>
> And Abraham said unto his eldest servant of his house, that ruled over all that he had, Put, I pray thee, thy hand under my thigh:
>
> And I will make thee swear by the Lord, the God of heaven, and the God of the earth, that thou shalt not take a wife unto my son of the daughters of the Canaanites, among whom I dwell:
>
> But thou shalt go unto my country, and to my kindred, and take a wife unto my son Isaac.
>
> And the servant took ten camels of the camels of his master, and departed; for all the goods of his master were in his hand: and he arose, and went to Mesopotamia (Genesis 24:1-4, 10).

In studying the historical records of the Old Testament, we must first of all remember that underneath and behind every record is some great spiritual truth and lesson. The Bible was not written primarily to record the history of certain men or nations or incidents, or to teach us moral and ethical lessons alone. All these things we are told were for our admonition:

> Now all these things happened unto them for ensamples: and they are written for our admonition, upon whom the ends of the world are come (I Corinthians 10:11).

And Paul in writing to Timothy declares in II Timothy 3:16, 17:

> All scripture is given by inspiration of God, and is profitable for doctrine, for reproof, for correction, for instruction in righteousness:

> That the man of God may be perfect, throughly furnished unto all good works.

Behind and in every record in Scripture, therefore, there is more than a historical record, more than an interesting account and more than mere moral instruction. The first thing Paul mentions is "doctrine." We must look first of all for the doctrine, and then the reproof, the correction and instruction will follow. If our doctrine is wrong, then our instruction in life also will necessarily be wrong.

Genesis 24 contains a great doctrine, the doctrine of the ministry of the Holy Spirit of God. In this chapter we see the Trinity of God at work together. Abraham, as you recall, is a picture of the loving Father who withheld not His Own Son, but gave Him to die for us. Isaac is the son, obedient to death, while Eliezer, the elder servant of Abraham, corresponds to the Holy Spirit, sent by the father after the death and resurrection of the son to bring home the bride. In the opening verses of Genesis 24 we see a number of things foreshadowing the work of the Holy Spirit in this dispensation which positively identifies Eliezer as a picture of this Holy Spirit.

I.

"Eliezer" means God's helper. It comes from the fragment, *El*, the first syllable of one of the primary names of God, Elohim. The last three syllables signify help. He is, therefore, the one sent by Abraham to help Rebekah to come to her husband, Isaac. This is also the ministry of the Holy Spirit today, to help God's chosen to come to the Son of God. In Romans 8:26, He, the Spirit, is said to be our helper in our infirmities:

> Likewise the Spirit also helpeth our infirmities: for we know not what we should pray for as we ought: but the Spirit itself maketh intercession for us with groanings which cannot be uttered.

II.

Eliezer also was sent by Abraham the father in behalf of his son Isaac. In John 14:16, 17 Jesus says concerning the Holy Spirit:

> And I will pray the Father, and he shall give you another Comforter, that he may abide with you forever;
> Even the Spirit of truth.

Then again in verse 26 Jesus says this:

> But the Comforter, which is the Holy Ghost, whom the Father will send in my name, he shall teach you all things.

III.

Furthermore, Eliezer was given full and complete authority to administer the affairs of the son and to seek out the bride for Isaac. The record tells us that Eliezer "ruled over all that he [Abraham] had" (Genesis 24:2), and "all the goods of his master were in his hand" (Genesis 24:10). So too the Holy Spirit came with the full authority of deity. While Eliezer is called a servant, it does not mean that he was inferior in any way. Jesus also is called the "servant of the Lord" but that in no way detracts from His deity. He is a servant only in the sense of His work of saving us, just as the Holy Spirit also takes the role of a servant, but it does not detract from the fact that He is equal with God the Father and with God the Son.

IV.

In the fourth place, there was only one condition laid down; namely, the bride must not come from among the Canaanites, but from the family and kindred of Abraham. How clearly this is stated in verses 2 and 3 of chapter 24:

> Thou shalt not take a wife unto my son of the daughters of the Canaanites, among whom I dwell:
> But thou shalt go unto my country, and to my kindred, and take a wife unto my son Isaac.

The Canaanites were the descendants of Canaan, grandson of Noah, placed under the curse because of his father Ham's sin. She who is to be the bride of Isaac must be free from the curse. She is to be chosen from the seed of Shem, who was in the special blessing of Noah. The Bride of the Lord Jesus Christ also will be a foreknown, foreordained, elect company, by faith, free from the curse of the law, and under the blessing of Almighty God.

V.

Again, this bride must come from a far country to be brought to Isaac the son. By no means is the servant Eliezer to bring Isaac to the bride's land for the wedding. This Abraham definitely commanded Eliezer, as he says in verse 6 (after Eliezer asks what to do if the bride will not come):

> Beware thou that thou bring not my son thither [to Mesopotamia, the home of the bride] again.

This command is repeated again in verses 7 and 8 where Abraham says:

> Thou shalt take a wife unto my son from thence . . . only bring not my son thither again.

Surely the type is perfectly clear. When the Church as the Bride goes to meet Isaac, Isaac does not come to her home here on the earth to get her. Instead the Holy Spirit will bring her to meet Him in the air. Paul says of this Bride, the church:

> The dead in Christ shall rise first:
>
> Then we which are alive and remain shall be caught up together with them in the clouds, to meet the Lord *in the air* (I Thessalonians 4:16, 17).

VI.

A sixth point which identifies Eliezer as a type of the Holy Spirit is that there was a full agreement and understanding between Abraham the father and Eliezer the servant. Genesis 24:9 states:

> And the servant put his hand under the thigh of Abraham his master, and sware to him concerning that matter.

So too it is with the Holy Spirit today. The Apostle John is clear in telling us in John 16:13:

He shall not speak of himself; but whatsoever he shall hear,
that shall he speak.

It is the work of the Holy Spirit to speak the word of God
the Father concerning God the Son. This is why there is so
much about the Lord Jesus Christ in the New Testament,
and so comparatively little about the Holy Spirit himself.
Only so much as is needed for Him to fulfill His mission
in revealing the Son is given to us.

VII.

Next, notice where Eliezer went:

He went to Mesopotamia, unto the city of Nahor (Genesis 24:10).

This was in the land of the Ur of the Chaldees, from which
Abraham himself had come. You will recall that "Ur" means
"flame," and "Chaldee" means "destruction." "Mesopotamia"
means between the rivers, and "Nahor" signifies the snoring
of a sleeping man. Nahor, then, represents one who has fallen
asleep. Eliezer goes to seek a bride in a land of flame and
destruction, between two great rivers (also called floods) and
to a city of sleeping snorers. The Holy Spirit too has gone
into the world of sinners who are under judgment of fire and
who live in a land of destruction.

VIII.

A precious thing is said concerning Eliezer in the next
verse. He was a praying servant. When he came to the
country of the bride, we read:

And he said, O Lord God of my master Abraham, I pray
thee, send me good speed this day, and shew kindness unto
my master Abraham (Genesis 24:12).

We have already pointed out how the Spirit helps our infirmities because we know not what to pray for as we ought.
The Spirit Himself makes intercession for us.

IX

Finally, when Eliezer stopped to choose the bride he did so
at a well. He knew that in that thirsty land all had to come

to the well sooner or later. He therefore went directly to the place where Isaac's future bride was expected to come. How appropriate to seek a bride for Isaac at a well, for Isaac was the well digger among the four great patriarchs. While Abraham was always building altars, Isaac was constantly digging wells. It is at the well that the servant meets the bride, thirsty and tired and weary, yet willing to accept the invitation. Jesus, the greater than Isaac, is also the well digger of salvation. He came into a thirsty world, and said unto a miserable woman at the well in Samaria:

> Whosoever drinketh of this water shall thirst again:
>
> But whosoever drinketh of the water that I shall give him shall never thirst; but the water that I shall give him shall be in him a well of water springing up into everlasting life (John 4:13, 14).

Have you been to the well, my friend? After all, it is the practical application of these truths to your own heart which is of paramount importance. We are living in a world that is thirsting for something which the world itself cannot satisfy. Someone has said that this old world is thirsting indeed for God, but a round world cannot fill a three-cornered heart. As you know, our heart is triangular in shape. There is only One who can fill it, and that is the Trinity, Father, Son and Holy Spirit. The world can never satisfy. Man was created with a capacity for infinity, and nothing that the world can offer can ever satisfy the human heart completely. Every sinner needs this living water, offered by the Holy Spirit of God through the Word. To reject the Lord Jesus Christ as Saviour, to turn a deaf ear to the pleading of the Spirit, is to perish forever. We find that the Bible closes with the gracious invitation to give to all those who are thirsty, the water of life:

> And the Spirit and the bride say, Come. And let him that heareth say, Come. And let him that is athirst come. And whosoever will, let him take the water of life freely (Revelation 22:17).

CHAPTER TWENTY-FIVE

Here Comes the Bride

> And it came to pass, before he had done speaking, that, behold, Rebekah came out, who was born to Bethuel, son of Milcah, the wife of Nahor, Abraham's brother, with her pitcher upon her shoulder.
>
> And the damsel was very fair to look upon, a virgin, neither had any man known her: and she went down to the well, and filled her pitcher, and came up (Genesis 24:15, 16).

Here comes the bride, with a pitcher on her shoulder. In the previous chapter we saw Eliezer, the servant of Abraham, being sent by the father to a far couutry to seek out a bride for the son. Eliezer had set out with a host of servants and ten camels laden down with treasures and gifts and jewelry and precious things from Isaac for his future bride. Now he waits for her at the well. Imagine an oriental evening as the sun is setting, the wind has died down, and here at the well are ten camels quietly resting, kneeling by the well of water, while Eliezer and the servants wait for the bride to come in answer to Eliezer's prayer. And then she appears, a beautiful, pure, young woman by the name of Rebekah. Paying apparently no attention at all to these strangers resting at the well with the camels, she gracefully trips down the steps to the well, lets down her pitcher, and comes up with it brimful of cool and sparkling water.

No Mistaking the Bride

And now Eliezer the servant goes into action. He had asked the Lord for a token to guide him on his way. He had requested of the Lord that if the maiden would not only let him, a total stranger, drink from her pitcher, but also offer to give water to his camels, this would indicate that she was the one to be the bride. The record is worthy of our attention. In verses 13 and 14 we read Eliezer's prayer:

> Behold, I stand here by the well of water; and the daughters of the men of the city come out to draw water:
>
> And let it come to pass, that the damsel to whom I shall say, Let down thy pitcher, I pray thee, that I may drink; and she shall say, Drink, and I will give thy camels drink also: let the same be she that thou hast appointed for thy servant Isaac; and thereby shall I know that thou hast shewed kindness unto my master.

That was quite an order which Eliezer requested from the Lord. To expect a young maiden to give drink to a total stranger was one thing, but to have her volunteer to draw water for ten thirsty camels was quite another thing. It meant many, many trips to the well with her pitcher. And then remember, there were servants with Eliezer (Gen. 24:32). While they sat and looked on, Eliezer expected Rebekah to draw water for the camels.

I repeat, therefore, that this seemed like an impossible request; yet astonishing as it may seem, we read this record: As Rebekah came up out of the well

> The servant ran to meet her, and said, Let me, I pray thee, drink a little water of thy pitcher.
>
> And she said, Drink, my lord: and she hasted, and let down her pitcher upon her hand, and gave him drink.
>
> And when she had done giving him drink, she said, I will draw water for thy camels also, until they have done drinking (Genesis 24:17-19).

This is the bride for Isaac, a beautiful picture in type of the Bride of the Lord Jesus Christ. This is her, a virgin, fair, pure, willing and ready. There was no mistaking her at all on the part of Eliezer. She was the one. So, too, there is no question concerning who belongs to the Bride of the Lord

Jesus Christ. God knows who are His. Paul says in II Timothy 2:19:

> Nevertheless the foundation of God standeth sure, having this seal, The Lord knoweth them that are his. And, Let every one that nameth the name of Christ depart from iniquity.

Indeed, those

> whom he did predestinate, them he also called: and whom he called, them he also justified: and whom he justified, them he also glorified (Romans 8:30).

PREPARATION OF THE BRIDE

Notice the work of the Holy Spirit in preparing this bride for the question, on the answer to which would depend her whole destiny. After Eliezer was sure Rebekah was the bride we read:

> And it came to pass, as the camels had done drinking, that the man took a golden earring of half a shekel weight, and two bracelets for her hands of ten shekels weight of gold;
>
> And said, Whose daughter art thou? tell me, I pray thee: is there room in thy father's house for us to lodge in? (Genesis 24:22-23).

Earrings were given to her for her ears, bracelets for her hands and a question for her permission. When the Holy Spirit begins His work in calling the sinner into the Body of Christ, He begins by the way of the ear. We must hear before we can act. Paul tells us in Romans 10:14, 17:

> How shall they believe in him of whom they have not heard: and how shall they hear without a preacher?
>
> So then faith cometh by hearing, and hearing by the word of God.

The first thing is the hearing of faith. Paul asked the Galatian Christians whether they had received the Lord Jesus Christ by the words of the law or by the hearing of faith (Galatians 3:5).

The Bride must hear the message and the Word. When a priest was consecrated in Israel, oil and blood were applied first of all to the lobe of the right ear, then to the thumb of the right hand and then to the big toe of the right foot. First, hear and obey with the ear; then serve with the hand; and then walk with the feet. That is God's order always: believing, serving and walking. So it was in the case of Rebekah, the bride for Isaac. Eliezer gave her first of all the earrings for her ears, which speaks of faith in the Word of God. Then he gave her bracelets for her hands, which speaks of service after we have believed. Then comes a question concerning definite separation: leaving her home and making the long journey to the bridegroom's house. After she had received the earrings and heard, and the bracelets to serve, we read:

> And the damsel *ran* and told them of her mother's house these things (Genesis 24:28).

When we have heard His invitation, we too must serve and we too must run to tell others of our wonderful, glorious meeting with the blessed Holy Spirit. When we are willing to do this, others too will become definitely interested in the same Person whom we have learned to love.

THE SERVANT TALKS ABOUT THE SON

The story continues in verses 29 and 30:

> And Rebekah had a brother, and his name was Laban: and Laban ran out unto the man, unto the well.
>
> And it came to pass, when he saw the earring and the bracelets upon his sister's hands, and when he had heard the words of Rebekah his sister, saying, Thus spake the man unto me; that he came unto the man.

Thus the whole family became interested, and they invited this man in and began preparations for his lavish entertainment. But Eliezer refused until after he had told his mission. He rehearses the entire story from the very beginning to the very end. He talks about Abraham and he talks about Isaac. He extols the son; he presents his wealth, his loveliness and his beauty, and tells them of all his wonderful virtues and characteristics. All the time he says nothing about himself at all. (I would strongly urge at this point that you read carefully the whole of chapter 24 of Genesis, and then turn to

John 14:16-26 and John 16:7-15. You will be thrilled by
the striking parallel in these passages, and see how Eliezer
as he seeks the bride Rebekah is one of the most beautiful
pictures of the work and the ministry of the Holy Spirit.)
Eliezer just talks about Isaac, opening bag after bag of precious
treasures which were Isaac's own possessions and giving
presents lavishly from Isaac to the bride. He tells Rebekah
of the wonderful future she is facing with Isaac the lover
and the bridegroom. We cannot fail to see in all of this a
shadow of the Holy Spirit as Jesus speaks of Him in John
16, verses 13 and 14:

> Howbeit when he, the Spirit of truth, is come, he will guide
> you into all truth: for he shall not speak of himself . . .
> He shall glorify me: for he shall receive of mine, and shall
> shew it unto you.

This is the ministry of the Holy Spirit in this dispensation
in which we are living today. He takes the treasures of God's
wonderful Word, which reveals God's Son, the Lord Jesus
Christ, and shows them unto us. Then He requests us to
believe them and to go with Him to meet the Bridegroom at
the end of the way.

EVERY STEP OF THE WAY

Friend, you too must make that journey into eternity one
of these days. There is no escaping it. It may be far sooner
than you think. You too need a guide, a leader, one who
can lead you home to the Son and the Father's House; for
without Him you must be lost forever. Only as you are willing to say "yes" to the Spirit of God, and receive the Lord
Jesus Christ as your Lord and Saviour can you be saved. Trust
Him now; "believe on the Lord Jesus Christ, and thou shalt
be saved." The Holy Spirit himself offers to guide us and
to lead us and to provide for our every need and necessity. All
we have to do is to follow. First comes believing, then acting,
then following.

In this precious narrative which we shall continue in

the next chapter, we have first of all the bride (the Church) believing what Eliezer (the Holy Spirit) told her concerning Isaac (Jesus Christ) whom she was to marry. Then comes the decision. She is to make up her mind, whether she, on the bare testimony of this man's word and the treasures which he revealed to her, is willing to go. She had never seen Isaac. She had never met Eliezer before. But we find she is willing to take the evidence which she saw in the treasures revealed to her and in the word of his authority, and to go with him into a country which she had never before seen.

The Holy Spirit also provides every need for every step along the way. Eliezer had come thoroughly prepared with ten camels supplied with treasures and provender and everything which was needful for the journey. All Rebekah had to do was to listen to him, follow instructions, stay close by him, and do his bidding and his will. After all, the most carefree life is the Christian life. We can cast all our burdens upon Christ and depend upon the leading of the Holy Spirit to see us through to the end: for "he that hath begun a good work in you will perform it until the day of Jesus Christ" (Philippians 1:6).

CHAPTER TWENTY-SIX

The Royal Honeymoon

> And the servant brought forth jewels of silver, and jewels of gold, and raiment, and gave them to Rebekah: he gave also to her brother and to her mother precious things.
>
> And they did eat and drink, he and the men that were with him, and tarried all night; and they rose up in the morning, and he said, Send me away unto my master (Genesis 24:53, 54).

The engagement is finally announced and the wedding day is drawing nigh. We are nearing the close of the history of the patriarch, Abraham. He has sent his servant, Eliezer, to seek a bride for his son, Isaac. Now the bride is all ready and will soon be on her way home to meet her espoused husband. The whole story becomes a picture of salvation, and the calling out of the Church, the Bride of the Lord Jesus Christ, for His own glory. God the Father sent the Holy Spirit into the world to seek a Bride for Christ, the son of God, over nineteen hundred years ago. And after all these centuries the end is drawing near.

THREE ODD REQUESTS

Near the end of chapter 24 of Genesis we find Eliezer in the house of Rebekah. She has decided to go with the servant upon the testimony that he has given. Notice that her decision was a personal one. No one else could make it for her. We read:

> And they said, We will call the damsel, and enquire at her mouth.

> And they called Rebekah, and said unto her, Wilt thou go with this man? And she said, I will go (vss. 57, 58).

This was the simple decision which Rebekah made, fully convinced in her own mind that she was doing the thing which was right. Permit me to remind you what it was that Rebekah was asked to do. There are just three things which stand out in the narrative:

1. She was asked to go with a person she never knew before.
2. She was asked to marry a man whom she had never met.
3. She was asked to leave her home and go to a country she had never seen before, and from which she might never return.

Despite these three conditions, she said, "I will go," and that settled it. It was faith, simple, absolute, trusting faith in the word of Eliezer which was supported by the treasures of Isaac which Eliezer had brought along.

So, too, the only way that sinners can be saved today is by that same simple faith in the Spirit's Word, and in the treasures of God's wonderful Book. God asks us to believe the Holy Spirit and His testimony and the Word of God, though we have never known Him before; to put our trust in the Saviour whom we have never seen and never met; and to trust our destiny to this Guide who will take us to a heaven where we have never been. Salvation is by simple faith, and faith alone. How wonderfully Peter expresses it in I Peter 1:8:

> Whom having not seen, ye love; in whom, though now ye see him not, yet *believing*, ye rejoice with joy unspeakable and full of glory.

A Wonderful Guide

Rebekah prepares herself and places herself in the complete care of this servant, Eliezer:

> And Rebekah arose, and her damsels, and they rode upon

the camels, and *followed the man*: and the servant took Rebekah, and went his way (Genesis 24:61).

Rebekah followed the man, for he alone knew the way. He acted as a guide, protector, entertainer and sustainer all along the long, tedious journey to her husband, Isaac. In this connection we should read carefully John 16:12-15. Here Jesus is speaking of the blessed Holy Spirit so clearly foreshadowed by Eliezer, and says:

I have yet many things to say unto you, but ye cannot bear them now.

Howbeit when he, the Spirit of truth, is come, *he will guide you* into all truth: for he shall not speak of himself; but whatsoever he shall hear, that shall he speak: and he will shew you things to come.

He shall glorify me: for he shall receive of mine, and shall shew it unto you.

All things that the Father hath are mine: therefore said I, that he shall take of mine, and shall shew it unto you.

These are the words of our precious Lord and Saviour Jesus Christ Himself concerning the ministry of the Holy Spirit in this dispensation.

As we go back to Eliezer and Rebekah, we notice them on their journey. The trip is long and wearisome for Rebekah, but all the way the servant encourages her with more information about Isaac and his glory and his wealth and all of his beauty. At the eventide as they sit about the camp fire and the servants have retired, he tells her still more and opens up some more of the bags of Isaac's treasures (remember that there were ten camels laden down with these treasures for the bride). Every night he shows her new treasures, more beautiful than before; and all day as he guides her on the way, he speaks of Isaac and tells her of the things to come. He glorifies the son, and speaks not of himself.

That is exactly what the Holy Spirit does today. He witnesses with our spirits that we are the children of God. He tells us about the Son, Jesus Christ, and all His glory, and His wonderful Word. As we travel along, He opens up again and again and again new bags of treasures from this precious Word, new wonders from the Book, until we become so anxious to see Him, that it seems we cannot stand it any longer. As we travel along and study this Book, and listen to the Spirit, we learn more and more about *Him*; and our love for Him increases and grows. One of these days, suddenly, we too shall see Him as He comes to meet us.

The End of the Journey

That is the way the story of the bride ends in Genesis 24. How many days the journey lasted from Mesopotamia all the way to Isaac's home, we do not know. But one day,

> Isaac came from the way of the well Lahairoi; for he dwelt in the south country.
>
> And Isaac went out to meditate in the field at eventide: and he lifted up his eyes, and saw, and, behold, the camels were coming (vss. 62, 63).

Isaac had undoubtedly gone into the field to meditate about his coming bride, to look for the return of Eliezer and Rebekah. At long last, behold, the camels were coming, carrying the bride. At the same time Rebekah saw Isaac afar off also:

> And Rebekah lifted up her eyes, and when she saw Isaac, she lighted off the camel.
>
> For she had said unto the servant, What man is this that walketh in the field to meet us? And the servant had said, It is my master: therefore she took a veil, and covered herself.
>
> And the servant told Isaac all things that he had done (vss. 64-66).

How unfathomly rich, how inexpressibly precious, is this wonderful, tender scene. When Rebekah saw Isaac she alighted from the camel. Undoubtedly she recognized him, and now her traveling days are done. Her carriage on this long journey through the wilderness was no more needed. She covered her face in adoration and worship before her lover.

Today we as believers are almost to this very point in our journey. For nineteen hundred years the Holy Spirit has been here gathering out the Bride and guiding her on her way home. Soon, yes, we believe very soon, we too will one day lift up our eyes, and lo and behold, Jesus our lover, our Saviour, will break through the clouds to meet us; and we, like Rebekah, lighting from the camel of mortality, will leave our earthly vehicle and rise to meet Him in the air with glorified bodies.

> The Lord himself shall descend from heaven with a shout, with the voice of the archangel, and with the trump of God: and the dead in Christ shall rise first:
>
> Then we which are alive and remain shall be caught up together with them in the clouds, to meet the Lord in the air: and so shall we ever be with the Lord (I Thessalonians 4:16, 17).

With all my heart I believe that day is almost here.

The story ends as a real story book ends: they live happily forever after. Here is the close of the tender, touching scene:

> And Isaac brought her into his mother Sarah's tent, and took Rebekah and she became his wife; and he loved her; and Isaac was comforted after his mother's death. (vs. 67).

Now we draw the tent flap and leave the happy honeymooners to themselves. Notice that Isaac brought Rebekah into his mother's tent. Sarah, we have already seen, was the mother who gave birth to the man child, to the son. She represents Israel, the nation set aside and buried among the other nations while the bride is being brought home. Rebekah represents the Church who now enters Sarah's tent, and becomes with Israel, partaker of the blessing of Abraham. This is what Paul refers to in Romans 11 when he speaks of the olive tree (Israel) whose branches were broken off in order that the Church might be grafted into the stump of Abraham, and with Israel become a partaker of the root and fatness of the olive tree (Romans 11:13-24).

The bride is home at last, and we leave them in the tent by themselves. One of these days, our Lover, our Bridegroom, the Lord Jesus, will behold the camels coming and come to meet us, and take us to the place He promised when He said,

> Let not your heart be troubled: ye believe in God, believe also in me.
>
> In my Father's house are many mansions: if it were not so, I would have told you. I go to prepare a place for you.
>
> And if I go and prepare a place for you, I will come again, and receive you unto myself; that where I am, there ye may be also (John 14:1-3).

AFTER THE WEDDING

Abraham remarries and raises a large family, in fulfillment of God's promise that in him all nations of the earth would be blessed, and that his seed would be like the dust of the earth. After the rapture and the wedding of the Lamb in the sky, Jesus will come to this earth with His Bride to set up His Kingdom. In Him shall all the nations of the earth be blessed and Abraham's covenant will be completely fulfilled. God will then, as He tells us in Micah 4:3 and 4, cause men to

> Beat their swords into plowshares, and their spears into pruninghooks: nation shall not lift up a sword against nation, neither shall they learn war any more.
>
> But they shall sit every man under his vine and under his fig tree; and none shall make them afraid: for the mouth of the Lord of hosts hath spoken it.

With that thought we conclude this book on Abraham's adventures in faith. May God use it to cause many to heed the pleadings of the Holy Spirit and be saved. May we as believers lift up our eyes on high, and look for Him who is almost at the door. One of these days we will say to the Holy Spirit, "Who is that?" and He will say as Eliezer said to Rebekah, "That's Him." Instead of lighting from the camel, we will rise up in the sky, for the Lord Himself will call us home to meet Him. We do not know when this meeting will be, but we know it is coming. Then we will pull the tent flap shut, and be ever with the Lord.

It may be at morn, when the day is awaking,
When sunlight through darkness and shadow is breaking,
That Jesus will come in the fulness of glory,
To receive from the world "His own."

It may be at midday, it may be at twilight,
It may be, perchance, that the blackness of midnight
Will burst into light in the blaze of His glory,
When Jesus receives "His own."

Oh, joy! oh, delight! should we go without dying;
No sickness, no sadness, no dread, and no crying,
Caught up in the clouds with our Lord into glory,
When Jesus receives "His own."

Surely, our hearts do cry out:
O Lord Jesus, how long, how long
Ere we shout the glad song,
Christ returneth? Hallelujah, hallelujah! Amen.
Hallelujah! Amen.

He which testifieth these things saith, Surely I come quickly.
Amen. Even so, come, Lord Jesus.

The grace of our Lord Jesus Christ be with you all. Amen
(Revelation 22:20, 21).